THE REAL TREASURE – VI

Life of A Resident

With

Avatar Meher Baba's Mandali

© **Rustom B. Falahati**

Dedication

I dedicate this book to **Beloved Avatar Meher Baba** who is the **"Being of all beings."**

Acknowledgments

I am indebted to Beloved Avatar Meher Baba's Mandali for the stories that made "The Real Treasure" series possible. I thank Baba's Mandali namely Bhauji and Meheru for they were the ones who encouraged me to continue writing during my last meeting with them. For the writing of this present volume I express my gratitude to Meherwan Jessawala whose help and guidance made it possible.

A special thanks to my loving wife Meher without whose help none of the volumes would have seen the light of the day. A heartfelt thanks to Steve Klein who not only edited all the volumes but was also there to guide me whenever I needed directions. I thank Cyrus, Soumya and Craig Ruff for being there for me. I thank Ganesh, Shalini and Nitin for proof reading this book. Last but not the least I thank the entire team of loyal friends, who stood by me and supported me in every aspect of this most precious Baba work.

As I stand before Baba my Lord, my God, I have no words to express my gratitude my indebtedness to my Creator. He has led me by holding my hand every step of the way. From being an atheist who loved aggression to someone who spreads His message of Love and Truth to His lovers through "The Real Treasure' is something only He can do. He alone is the only doer of all things. He alone IS.

Table of Contents

Introduction

It was on 15th August 2012 that I phoned Bhauji. My health was very bad at that time and I was unable to bear it. I phoned with the intent of requesting him to pray to Baba to relieve me from this unbearable suffering. Bhauji has often explained to us that one who longs for God should be prepared for total ruination and whatever suffering comes his way, he should bear it cheerfully. To ask for relief from such suffering would mean a spiritual setback for the aspirant. You have to sacrifice one for the sake of the other. On that day when I phoned Bhauji, he more or less talked on similar lines and then asked me to choose. I was confused and it dawned on me that it was best to resign to Baba's will and let Him decide. I recorded this whole incident the same day and it was used as a final story of Vol. 5 "The Real Treasure."

The very next morning we got news that Eruch Jessawala's sister Manu passed away into Baba. By noon my health deteriorated and I could not bear the discomfort. Not in a position to go and visit a doctor, we decided to call the local doctor home for checkup. The doctor agreed to come at 7 pm. My physical discomfort kept increasing and I fainted by 6:30 pm. When the doctor visited, on finding me unconscious, he suggested that I be shifted to the hospital immediately. An ambulance was called and I was admitted to the I.C.U. (intensive care unit) of Prince Ali Khan Hospital. I had a high fever and was diagnosed with a urinary tract infection, and a sodium deficiency.

The next day I regained consciousness, however I would experience intense tremors through the day. Also, my body would stiffen up at times causing intense pain. I was told that these were the side effects of low sodium. I was conscious for the most part but there were times I would become delirious and incoherent in my speech, losing awareness of everything. This too being the side effect of sodium deficiency but, strangely enough, the doctor attributed it to a mental disturbance. After a few days, the doctor felt that I should be shifted to a psychiatric ward. As the hospital did not have a psychiatric ward, I was shifted to another one called Masina hospital.

What happened after that was a frightening nightmare – a tale of medical horror. The psychiatrist roped in a physician and an orthopedic. The very next day, I fainted again and was admitted to I.C.U. The physician treated me for low sodium and also informed the other doctors that my condition was physical. The orthopedic on the other hand did not carry out any elaborate tests to find out the cause of the intense pain in my body. Only an X-ray was taken. As the X-ray showed minor problems, he concluded that my condition was mental and I was imagining pain. I was put on psychiatric medicines. The side effect of the medicine was horrendous. I was feeling drowsy most of the time and for the most part not aware of what transpired during my stay in this hospital. The hospital branded me a mental case and appointed a ward boy (attendant) to keep an eye on me – this being a normal procedure for mental patients. Most of the ward boys are illiterate youth from rural areas, who are given a very basic and limited training in handling patients. They treat everyone in the psychiatric ward as mad and handle them very roughly.

The only memory I have of my stay in this hospital was of Bhauji and Meherwan phoning me daily to inquire about my health and reminding me to remember Baba. When my health stabilized, I was shifted from I.C.U. to the psychiatric ward. After a few days of treatment, the psychiatrist decided to give me shock treatment to speed up my healing. For this he needed my family's consent, which my wife refused. My wife pointed out to the doctor that my body was frail as I had lost a lot of body weight and I would not be able to bear it. My body weight was 45 Kg which was 15 Kg below normal. The psychiatrist was persistent and assured my wife that nothing would happen. My wife requested time to think it over after consulting all family members. She contacted some Baba lover friends who were in the medical profession and they all suggested to her to follow the psychiatrist's advice. My wife Meher consented reluctantly.

The next day I was taken for administering the treatment. I was put under anesthesia so I do not know what happened after that. However, when I regained consciousness, I was in excruciating pain. The doctor ignored my complaints calling it my imagination. It was only when my family pressured him that he decided to do an X-ray. The X-ray revealed that both my hip joints were fractured by the shock treatment. My family members were horrified. They contacted an orthopedic, who had treated many of our family members, for help. After hearing what had happened, the orthopedic advised that I be removed from the Masina hospital immediately and be brought to Hinduja Hospital where he worked. When my family approached the psychiatrist for a discharge, he refused. It was only when he was threatened with litigation that he relented.

On admission to Hinduja Hospital, the orthopedic appointed a team of doctors to study my case. He roped in a physician, a neurologist and a psychiatrist. Elaborate tests were carried out. After examining the reports the orthopedic informed my family that apart from both my hip joints, my left shoulder was fractured and the nerves of my left legs were damaged. He looked at the reports in disbelief. Nodding his head from side to side he said, "All this was unnecessary suffering. You should have brought him earlier to me. Why did you take him to Masina? It was a simple case that has been made so complicated. In fact his bone density test shows he has severe osteoporosis with high fracture risk. The treatment damaged him severely."

The other doctors on the team also studied my case. It was the neurologist who pointed to one of the medicines that I was taking and to Meher he said, "This particular medicine is known to cause hallucinations. This, along with low sodium, is the cause of your husband's strange behavior. We have to wean him away from it gradually or else it may also cause reaction. When we stop it completely, he will be normal."

On the day of the operation the orthopedic explained to me that he would operate on one hip and only if my frail body could withstand the strain then he would operate on the second one. By Baba's Grace both hips were operated upon. I was becoming more and more aware of my surroundings and what was going on around me. As part of my rehabilitation, physiotherapy was started. At this point, I realized that I was forgetting everything that I did through the day. I discussed this with my psychiatrist who told me that it was a short term memory loss which often accompanied shock treatment and it would pass. My long term memory was intact and I remembered my past clearly but I could not remember anything I did through the day.

If the visiting doctor asked me questions such as,

"Did you take your medicine or has the lab report come, etc." I would not remember, so I would not reply. Fortunately for me, Meher was by my side all the time and she would answer. Although the psychiatrist assured me that my memory would come back slowly, I was terribly frightened. I had become so completely helpless and over dependent on Meher that if she left my side even for a short while, I would feel anxious. On a few occasions when the doctors arrived, Meher was not around. My reply to their queries on such occasions was, "I don't know, my wife knows, she can tell you."

I was discharged after ten days. At home we hired an attendant to help me. A physiotherapist visited daily to help me with my exercises. I asked my wife to memorize the exercises and also to remind me about all the things that I was supposed to do through the day. As time passed, my memory improved and so also my body weight. In two months' time I was able to walk independently, something I had not done in the last seven years. My body weight became normal during this period. All my friends and family were happy at the development.

However, I was suffering internally which no one could see because it was internal. It wasn't the constant pain in my hip that bothered me. What troubled me most was the fact that the fiery presence of Baba, which I felt all these years had vanished from my heart. It was this presence that sustained me during my years of incapacities. It was this presence that wrote "The Real Treasure" which helped me so immensely. The presence had left me; it completely disappeared. I felt like an empty shell. I performed my daily tasks like an automation taking no interest in anything. The fire inside me had died out and with it my inner being had died too.

Meher noticed it and tried to encourage me in different ways. She would call up Bhauji and Meherwan from time to time and make me talk with them. I would do it reluctantly. Meherwan sensed it too and asked me to start writing again. I explained to him my inability to do it without His presence. Meherwan persisted by saying, "Start writing. His presence is always there. He will write it as He did earlier. The flow of stories will start." Under pressure I wrote a couple of stories but the flow did not happen. I gave up the thought of writing completely. Without the presence guiding me I knew it was futile, for I was not a writer.

After six months I was able to do most of the things independently and my memory was more or less normal. I decided to start going to the Bombay Centre in the hope that my inner state would change. Meher and I would attend the book reading sessions and the story sharing sessions every week. Book reading conducted by Cyrus Khambata on Tuesdays and storytelling sessions conducted on Thursdays by Sam Patel. They would often invite me to share stories. I would refuse citing bad health. On one occasion Sam turned to my wife Meher and asked her to share stories of her dad, Keki Desai's life with Baba. Meher, being shy was hesitant but, with a little prompting from me and other lovers, she agreed. Everyone loved the stories she shared. When she finished, Sam said to me, "You should write these stories in your future volumes." I told him that my writing days were over and I was finished with writing. As time passed by, I too started sharing stories. When Baba lovers had doubt and they would ask question, I would share stories to clarify the point.

It was during the Baba birthday celebration in the year 2014 at the Bombay Centre that Cyrus invited me to share my experiences with Baba lovers who would be attending the programme. I expressed my reluctance to him. Cyrus was persistent. He said to me, "The crowd will be basically the same that you meet every week with a few extra faces, whom you already know. In the past, you avoided our invitation due to bad health, but your health is okay now. So what is your reason for refusing, let us know and we will help you?" Under pressure from Meher and my Mom, I agreed. I was given a slot of one and half hours to share the stories.

The programme went well and everyone enjoyed it. It was recorded by a Baba lover and put on the internet. Rakhi Sharma -- a Baba lover who lives in Delhi -- happened to see it on the net. Rakhi has been conducting the Young Adult Baba Sahavas at Meherabad for many years. Every year she would invite me to share stories with the Sahavasees. I would turn it down on grounds of bad health. When she came to know of the Bombay Centre programme, she phoned me up. She was very emphatic that I attend the Young Adult Sahavas and share Baba stories. I had no choice but to agree. It was a nice experience addressing the Sahavasees and sharing stories of the Mandali as it brought me out of my shell. After the Sahavas was over, I decided to stay back in order to spend time with Meherwan.

I decided to go early to Meherazad before the Trust bus arrived with the pilgrims. That way I could spend some private moments with Meherwan. On reaching Meherazad, we took Baba's darshan and then greeted Meherwan who was seated on the verandah. Meherwan made us sit next to him and inquired after our wellbeing. After we chatted for a while, Meherwan asked me, "Do you go to the Bombay Centre?" I said to him that we did and added. "These days even Meher shares stories of her dad Keki's life with Baba, and Baba lovers enjoy it." Meherwan appeared pleased and said, "That's good." He then turned to me and said, "You should write these stories down in your next volume." I don't know why but Meherwan's words struck my heart as a lightning and ignited the fire again. I found myself muttering to him, "If He so wishes, it will happen."

Meherwan proceeded to tell me that Keki Desai was very fortunate as he got the opportunity to serve and live with Baba during the New Life phase – when no one was allowed to see or contact Baba. Meherwan added, "Baba will write it. All you have to do is invite Him and become a willing instrument".

When I reached home, I picked up the pen and started writing. The stories began to flow out. I could feel the presence again. It wasn't the fiery presence that I had felt over the years, but a gentle fire that helped me complete this volume. The reader will find this volume different from all the other volumes. It consists of two sections. The first section, as in the previous volumes, consists of accounts of the Mandali's interaction with the residents. The second section consists of an account of Keki Desai's life with Baba. This was compiled by combining notes which Keki had made with Meher's remembrance of stories which she had heard her dad tell over the years. Rather than present it as one long account, I have broken it up into many small sections, even when the sections don't make up a "story" as such. I hope the reader finds this section enjoyable and instructive. As Meherwan conveyed, it is a rare glimpse into Baba's activities during the New Life.

If the reader is wondering whether there will be another volume after this, my reply to it is the same as before. I have no more stories to write about, but if He so wishes then it will happen.

HOW BABA CREATES LOVE

I met Sam Kerawala when I first went to live at Meherabad as a resident. He has been a great story-teller and would captivate the audience with stories of his interactions with Baba. In addition to this, he would even share Sufi stories he had read and memorized. He and his entire family had a very close and intimate relationship with Baba. Knowing this, I once asked Sam, "At what point in time in your life did you begin to feel and perceive Baba as God? There are many Baba lovers like you who were born in Baba families, however, their conviction that Baba is God came only years later and in some cases it did not come at all." Sam replied, "I was born into a family that was totally dedicated to Baba. As a child, my parents introduced Baba as God to me and made me pray to Him. We had full faith in our parents and accepted whatever they said as a matter of fact."

I asked him another question. "We hear many stories of how Baba needled His lovers and often that created a doubt in their minds about His divinity. Did you ever have any such experience around Baba?" Sam replied, "I never ever had any doubts about Baba's divinity. However, there is one particular story which comes to mind about Baba needling me."

Sam proceeded to share the following story. "You know I have a brother Dadi Kerawala whom you have already met. On one occasion, when we were both with Baba attending His Sahavas, He turned to me and said, 'Sam you love Me but I love Dadi.' I smiled at Baba and said with a nod, 'Baba whatever you say.' The next day again when we were with Him, Baba turned to me and repeated what He had said the previous day. 'Sam you love Me but I love Dadi.' I smiled again and nodded in affirmation. When Baba continued doing this for several days, I began to feel upset at the fact that Baba did not love me. He only loved Dadi. I had no idea what needed to be done by me to win over His love. So one day when Baba said the same thing again, I mustered the courage and asked Him, 'Baba why is it that you only love Dadi and not me? What is it that I have to do to win over Your love?' Baba smiled and said to me with great affection, 'It's not as you think. You already have love for Me in your heart whereas Dadi does not have it. So I have to love him, for that will create love in his heart for Me. Because of My love for him, some day he will be able to love Me the way you love Me.'"

"When I heard Baba say that, all the upset feeling in my heart, which I was experiencing for the last few days, disappeared and I felt happy."

CENTER OF UNIVERSE

A Baba lover from Pakistan had come for Baba's Guruprasad programme. She had met Baba on several occasions, but this was the first time she had come for a programme where such a large number of Baba lovers had assembled. The following is her story in her own words.

"I was standing in queue eagerly awaiting my turn to take Baba's darshan. Baba's face was glowing like the sun and He was looking Divinely radiant. When my turn came for taking darshan, Baba showered His attention on me by enquiring about my family, their wellbeing and also about my health. He then asked me, 'Have you met the ladies?' By ladies Baba meant the lady Mandali members. I said, 'No Baba.' Baba asked me to go and meet them.

"As I was leaving to go meet the ladies, Baba clapped and called me. He enquired, 'Where is your purse?' Pointing towards my seat I said to Baba, 'I have left it on my seat.' Baba said with a look of concern on His face, 'Do not leave it there, take it with you or it might get stolen.' I laughed and said to Baba, 'Who would steal in Your darbar. Why would a thief come to your darbar to steal?'

"With a look of seriousness Baba said, 'I am the Centre of Universe. I attract both the positive and the negative. You will find the greatest saint and the biggest scoundrel in My darbar. They get naturally attracted to Me as I am their Real Self. So do not be careless about your personal belongings, just because you are in My presence, for it can get stolen.' I thanked Baba and went to my seat, picked up my purse and went to meet the lady Mandali Members." She then added, "Whenever I see a pilgrim being careless about her personal belongings during the pilgrimage to Meherabad, I share this story with them as a warning to be careful."

MAST

We would often accompany Bhauji to Poona for Trust work. On one such trip, after the work was over and we were returning, one of the residents asked the driver of the car to slow down when we reached an open space on the Pune-Nagar road. The resident then pointed towards a man in tattered clothes and asked Bhauji. "Is that man over there a mast? I believe Erico showed him to you and you seemed to agree." Bhauji turned to look at the man who was seated on a patch of wild congress grass by the side of the road and replied, "Yes. He is the one that Erico showed me and I feel he is a mast." The resident then asked Bhauji, "Did Erico share his story of his meeting with the mast?" Bhauji replied, "Yes he did." The resident added, "It was an amazing encounter."

Since I did not know the story, I requested the resident to narrate it for me. The resident narrated the following story. "Erico happened to be walking on the street which we just passed. He noticed some street urchins troubling the man in tattered clothes. They would call him mad and often throw stones at him. As you know, Erico speaks fluent Hindi and Marathi. So he yelled at the street urchins in Hindi threatening and abusing them simultaneously. The kids were frightened by the sight of this big westerner abusing them in Hindi and ran away. Erico then went up to that man and asked him if he wanted some food. The man nodded. Erico brought some food and fed him.

"In interacting with the man, Erico felt that he was a mast. Erico then went to a nearby store and brought a set of new clothes for the man. Erico changed the man's clothes after which the man went to lie down in an open patch of congress grass. For those who do not know, congress grass can cause allergic reactions such as itch and rash. Even animals do not consume it and destroying this weed is very difficult. However, it did not seem to bother the mast and he slept in it as if he was sleeping on a comfortable bed. Erico massaged the mast for some time and said to him, 'Baba, I have to go now. Is there anything at all that you need please tell me and I will get it for you?' The mast had both his hands locked under his head, using them as a pillow. He was staring at the sky when Erico asked him the question. Slowly he turned his head towards Erico and said to him, 'Kuch nahi chahiye muje. Sab kuch hai mere pas. Is jagah ka malik hu mai,' which means, 'I do not need anything. I have everything. I am the master of this place.' Erico then bade the mast farewell and left."

WILLING INSTRUMENTS

A humorous incident that happened between Mansari and Mani is as follows:

It so happened that a meeting was called by Mani to discuss the upkeep of Beloved Baba's Samadhi. All residents who were connected with the work were asked to attend. Mansari was in charge of the day to day running of the Samadhi affairs, so she was invited to attend. These meetings were held on Meherabad hill in the study hall or library to enable Mansari to attend, if she so desired. If the meetings were to be held elsewhere, Mansari would not be able to attend as Baba had ordered her not to cross the railway tracks. She was more or less confined to live on her side of the railway track. In spite of all these arrangements, Mansari would not attend the meetings as she considered it a waste of time. She preferred that Mani take the decisions and inform her later.

I happened to be with Mansari one day, when she said to me, "Mani is going to come today for the meeting." I asked her if I should leave. She said, "No, I don't go for the meetings even though Mani wants me to." After a while Mani came in to meet Mansari. They talked for a while and then Mani asked Mansari to attend the meeting. Mansari refused as usual. Mani said to Mansari in a lighter vein, "You must attend the meeting – it's a good thing. You see, 'By ourselves we can decide nothing, but we can all get together and decide that we can do nothing.'" When Mani finished, we all started laughing. Then on a more serious note Mani said, "You see, we all think that we are doing things, that we are making decisions. In reality He is the One doing it. He is the only doer. All that we can do is to become willing instruments for Him to use us as He wishes for His work. So we have to go about our daily task of performing our duty in such a way so as to allow Him to do His work through us. We can only do that if we become His completely."

Mani's statement reminded me of Kabir's couplet: "I reside in every heart, but no one notices Me. I am the One who does everything, but the credit goes to My slave and not to Me."

TERRIBLE SANSKARAS

The following story was narrated to me by a Baba lover who was an ex-sailor. He had the good fortune of being born in a close Baba lover's family. His entire family had the good fortune of having Baba's intimate Sahavas on many occasions. In fact they were so close to Baba that Baba often guided them in their personal life regarding major decisions.

This Baba lover once said to me, "It so happened that after I returned from my very first voyage at sea, Baba asked me to meet Him. When I met Baba, He inquired about my wellbeing, the voyage, the nature of my work etc. and other details. Eventually He asked me, 'Do you drink?' I said, 'Yes Baba.' Baba asked, 'How much do you drink in a day?' I replied, 'Baba about three to four pegs and sometimes even more.' Baba gestured disapprovingly and said, 'You can drink, but no more than two pegs a day.'"

"After that Baba made a gesture of a bangle around the wrist and asked, 'Have you womanized?' I replied, 'Yes Baba.' Baba asked 'How many women have you slept with?' I replied, 'I don't know how many, but Baba in every port I slept with a woman. Baba looked very unhappy and said, 'From now on you should stop womanizing.' With a very serious look on His face Baba said, 'You have incurred terrible sanskaras by your actions. Indulgence in such actions leads to terrible suffering and may even take several lifetimes to erase such sanskaras. I will have to say a special prayer for you and you have to be present.' I agreed and Baba set a particular date for the prayer and asked me to be present on that day."

"On the day Baba made me stand next to Him and He recited a prayer. When the prayer finished, Baba showed me a freshly washed handkerchief and asked, 'Is this handkerchief clean?' I said, 'Yes Baba, it looks clean.' Baba then said to me, 'If you hold this handkerchief against the light you will notice a faint oil stain still on it. Just as a major portion of the oil stain has been scrubbed clean, a faint trace still remains on the kerchief. So also it is with your sanskaras. I have wiped out a major portion of those terrible sanskaras, but a faint trace still remains. You will have to suffer it out.' With that Baba asked me to refrain from any such acts."

When the sailor finished narrating his story, I had a baffled look on my face. He noticed it and said to me, "It appears that you have some question to ask." I said, "Yes. I can't understand why Baba did not give you the order 'to not womanize' before the voyage began. That way you would not have taken on those terrible sanskaras in the first place. He has given such orders to many young Baba lovers who then never indulged. Why He did not give it to you?" The sailor reflected over the question and said, "What you say is correct. I never really thought about it and I don't have an answer to that."

I really wanted an answer that made sense, so one day I asked Eruch about it as he knew the man's story, Eruch gave the following reply, "In my opinion, Baba often creates a situation by putting His close ones through it in order to leave a message for posterity. The whole incident is a message from Baba for posterity to not indulge in promiscuous sex. The sanskaras incurred from it are so terrible that even if God were to try and wipe it out for you, a trace of it will still remain for which you will have to suffer."

NEVER DISPLEASE BABA

It was in the year 2010 that the following incident happened. I was living in the Trust Compound with my wife at that time. During one of our visits to Meherazad, while travelling on the bus ,we met a man by the name of Kunal Phiroze. He happened to be sitting next to us and he started talking by introducing himself. "I am Phiroze, the son of Phiroza, who happened to be Adi K. Irani's sister." We were both happy and surprised to have met Adi K. Irani's nephew. I asked him, "Are you a regular visitor to this place? We have never met before, so I was wondering." His reply took me by surprise. He said, "No, this is my first visit." What he said further amazed me. He added, "In fact, I know nothing about Meher Baba, because my mother never mentioned anything about Meher Baba to me. She only told me that she grew up in Ahmednagar in Khushru Quarters (Trust Compound) and that her dad was a prominent and respectable man in Ahmednagar. She also mentioned her family members with whom she had lost contact long back.

As I was in Nagar, I decided to visit Khushru Quarters and find out if any of my mother's family or friends were still alive. I then met Bhauji who received me with great warmth and love. He informed me about the passing away of all members of my mother's family. He then shared stories about Meher Baba and also about how Adi K. Irani served

Baba as His secretary till the very end. I started reading books about Meher Baba and find them interesting. Bhauji mentioned that I would be able to meet the remaining Mandali at Meherazad and so I am looking forward to it." He paused and then added, "I came looking for my mom's family and I found God."

I could not believe what I had just heard. To confirm that what I heard was correct, I asked him, "Your mom never told you anything about Meher Baba?" He replied, "No. When I go back I will ask her the reason for it." He asked me if I knew any stories regards his mother. Even though I had heard a few stories about her from the Mandali, I chose not to share with him because they were unpleasant. The Mandali never talked in great details about Phiroza. However, Mani did mention on few occasions that Phiroza had drifted away from Baba and had broken all ties with Him. When Phiroza was living in the Trust Compound with her family she would often indulge in things that Baba disapproved of. She was indulging in occult practices such as black magic. In spite of repeated warnings from Baba to stop it, she continued with it. Eventually, Baba cut off all ties with her and even prevented the Mandali from interacting with her.

It so happened that after Baba dropped His body, Phiroza visited Ahmednagar. She decided to visit Khushru Quarters and meet her childhood friends and Mandali. She saw Mani from a distance and approached her. Mani had one look at her and turned her face away. She went up to Mani and said, "It seems that all of you have forgotten me." Mani looked at her and said, "Phiroza, you are right. We have forgotten all those who have forgotten Him. We have nothing to do with those who have nothing to do with Him." Saying this Mani walked away.

Often young Baba lovers indulge in all kind of things, saying that Baba is God and it really doesn't matter what we do. He loves us and can never disapprove of us. I share this story with such lovers with a warning not to indulge in those things Baba disapproved of, especially occult practices. Quoting the Mandali I would tell them what they said on the subject. Even if you cannot please Baba, do not do the things that displease Him and never do those things which He forbade us to do.

HABIT – A STICKY THING

Addressing a crowd of pilgrims, Adi K. Irani said the following on remembering Baba. He said, "Many Baba lovers complain about the difficulty they experience in remembering Baba through the day. To them I would say that with a little practice it will become easy. Practice doing it until it becomes a habit. Once it becomes a habit, then even if you want to give it up, it will be difficult. Habit is such a sticky thing, it sticks with you till the end. You often find people complaining about how difficult it is to break a habit, especially a bad one. Same is true about a good habit or any kind of habit. So why not make a habit of remembering Him, so that it sticks with you till the very end."

Adi paused, then continued, "Do you know why I say habit is a sticky thing? Look at the alphabets of the word habit. Remove the alphabet 'H' and 'abit' remains. Remove the alphabet 'A' and 'bit' still remains. Again if you were to remove the alphabet 'B', you will find that 'it' still remains. Such a sticky thing habit is, no matter what you do 'it' remains till the very end. That is why I say, make a habit of remembering Him and it will stick with you till the very end."

READING BABA BOOKS

A pilgrim once said to Eruch, "I have been with Baba for many years and I have not read any Baba books. I don't feel there is any need to read books about Him in order to love Him. Do you have anything to say on this subject?"

Eruch was silent for what seemed like an eternity. He then turned towards the pilgrim and asked him, 'Have you ever been in love with a girl?" The pilgrim replied, "Yes and I am married to her." Eruch said with a smile, "It is such a nice feeling to be in love. Did you not try to find out about the likes and dislikes of the girl that you were in love with? Did you not try and find out all details about her before you married her – details such as where does she live? How many family members does she have? What food does she like? , etc.etc."

The pilgrim replied, "That's a natural thing to do, if you want to get into a relationship." Eruch explained by saying, "Exactly. When you love someone you try to find out the smallest details about the person. Not only that, but after finding out everything you can, you try your utmost to please the person by doing the things she likes. It is the nature of love to do it. Love compels you to do it. Is that what you did when you were in love? Did you not do all the above things in love?"

The pilgrim replied, "It's something that almost everyone would do." Eruch commented, "For worldly love we take so much trouble and make so much effort. How much more effort we should be willing to put in for the sake of Divine Love? It is the nature of Love that goads you to find out more and more about your Beloved. You say you love Baba, that He is your Beloved. Don't you want to know about His likes and dislikes? About what pleases Him? Don't you want to try and please Him the way you did with the girl you love? So unless you read about Him, how will you know what His pleasure is? And unless you know His pleasure, how will you go about pleasing Him?

Eruch was silent for a very long time allowing everyone to digest what he had just said. He then spoke very slowly, "You have no idea what great trouble Baba had to put Himself through just to dictate a single sentence. Have you seen the movie, "Beyond Words" by Louie Van Gasteren? In that movie you can see Baba is gesturing to me and I am interpreting. His health was very bad at that time and even gesturing would cause Him pain, but He did it. He would gesture one letter at a time which I would repeat till the word was formed. Often I would get the word wrong or the letter wrong. Baba would signal to me that I was wrong and patiently re-dictate the whole thing till I got it right. You can see in the film how time consuming it was for Baba to dictate even a small sentence. Imagine how tedious the process of dictating a whole book must have been. Why did He put Himself through so much trouble? For our sake, so that we may read His messages and benefit from it by applying them to our lives. What made Him do all these things for us? It was His love for us. As I said before love compels you to do it. That's how it is. If He went through so much trouble because of His love for us, it behooves us as His lover to take the trouble and return that love back to Him."

JAI BABA OR JAI MEHER BABA

It was recently brought to my notice that an unnecessary controversy has been created in some of the Baba community regarding remembering Baba. Some feel that while taking His name one should say only 'Baba' and not say 'Meher Baba.' Whereas some others insist that it's always better to say 'Meher Baba' and not just 'Baba.' The same controversy surrounds the simple greeting that Baba lovers often use. Which greeting is correct 'Jai Baba' or 'Jai Meher Baba?'

When I was asked by some of the new lovers to comment on this, I shared with them all that the Mandali had said on the subject. In response to a question asked by a pilgrim in Meherazad Mandali Hall, whether one could repeat 'Meher Baba' instead of 'Baba,' Mani replied, "Why not? If your heart prompts you to do that, then do it. He is your Beloved and it does not matter by which name you call Him. As long as it's from the heart, He will always respond, for He knows you are calling Him. He hears the cry of the heart."

The pilgrim still had doubts and said to Mani, "In most of the books where Baba asks His lovers to repeat His name, He tells them to say, 'Baba, Baba . . .'" Mani replied promptly, "Yes that's true but has He said that you cannot say 'Meher Baba.' In fact the mechanical repetition of His name is just the beginning, which eventually leads to remembrance. In remembrance you are thinking of your Beloved day and night without uttering a word."

Mani then paused for a while and added, "You see, by asking us to say 'Baba, Baba,' He has not only made it easy for His lovers but also for those who do not know of Him. Let's say, if a person is following a different master. In India most masters are addressed as Baba. It does not matter who the master is as long as the disciples while calling out to their master say 'Baba,' they will reap the benefit of His name. In addition to the benefit rendered by Meher Baba to all these unknowing souls, there are many communities in India who address a child as 'Baba' or dad as 'Baba.' So, one calling out to a child or one's dad by the name 'Baba' benefits. Baba the all compassionate one has extended the benefit of His name to all these souls too."

On completing, Mani was silent. Everyone was trying to grasp the significance of what Mani had just said. In the meantime a pilgrim walked into the hall and greeted Mani with a 'Jai Baba.' Mani replied spontaneously, 'Baba Khodaiji.'

Khodaiji means God in Gujarati. It's the way Mani would greet Baba lovers, saying 'Baba is God.' Those of us who were around her knew it and we would reciprocate by saying 'Baba Khodaiji.' Commenting about it, Mani said, "This is how I greet people. It's personal." She then added, "Do you know Khorshed who lives in the Trust Office Compound? She greets everyone with 'Jai Meher Baba.' It's her way of greeting. Then there is Mansari who lives on Meherabad Hill. She greets everyone by saying 'Baba Nigeban,' which means 'Baba's sight is on you.' It's such a nice way to greet someone."

After pausing for a while Mani added, "By the way, the practice of greeting 'Jai Baba' was started by Pukar. He was a follower of Lord Ram. It's a common practice among Ram's followers to greet one another with 'Jai Ramji Ki' or 'Jai Ram.' When he became convinced that Baba is Lord Ram come again, he switched over from 'Jai Ram' to 'Jai Baba.' Mani concluded, "In your personal relationship with your Beloved, you call out to Him by the name that is dear to your heart. The longing and love behind the call is what matters."

SAY "O BELOVED" FROM THE HEART

When Eruch was asked for his opinion on whether one should say 'Baba' or 'Meher Baba' while repeating His name, Eruch replied, "If the longing and love is intense, then just a cry of 'O Beloved' from the heart is enough." He paused for a long time and then proceeded, "However, we don't have that kind of love or longing. So we have to begin by repeating His name. Whether you say 'Baba' or 'Meher Baba' or choose to repeat any of the 101 names of God, it's up to you. What is important is that you repeat any one name of God continuously throughout the day."

Eruch stopped for a while, allowing the pilgrims to digest the significance of what he had just said. He then proceeded, "Do you know what name of God Baba's father Sheriarji would repeat? He would repeat, 'Yazdan' continuously throughout the day. Sheriarji was the first to recognize Baba as the Awakener. The moment Baba was born, Sheriarji knew that the child was the One who had come to deliver the world. Even when Baba was a child, when He would enter the room, Sheriarji would stand up in reverence. Such was his love and devotion to Baba. Yet he repeated the name of Yazdan. He was such a great soul that Baba Himself said about him, 'There is none like him in the whole universe, he is matchless.' He did get God-realization upon dropping his body even though he was saying Yazdan and not Baba."

After a while, Eruch proceeded to give another example. "You all have heard about Gadge Maharaj, haven't you? He was a genuine 6th Plane saint and had come for the Wadia Park Darshan. He met Baba there and recognized Him as the Avatar. He later invited Baba to visit Pandharpur, which Baba did. At Pandharpur he proclaimed Baba as God to the villagers who were his followers and asked them to bow down to Baba. Even though he was a genuine saint, he would not allow anyone to bow down to him. In order to stop people from bowing down, he carried a stick which was 'V' shaped at the top. If anyone tried to bow down to him, he would push the stick and grab the person by the throat with it, pushing him up. Such a great soul. Do you know what name of God he would chant? In fact he would sing it all the time, 'Gopala, Gopala, Devekey Nandan Gopala.' They are all different names by which Lord Krishna was called. When he passed away, Baba said, 'Gadge Maharaj has come to Me.' Baba had promised Gadge Maharaj that He would call him to live with Him forever. Baba did honour His promise in a different way . . . by giving him God-realization. So you see, it's not important which name of God you take. After all they are all names by which He is called."

Allowing the pilgrims to digest what he had just said, Eruch stopped and was silent for a long time. Giving more examples to prove a point he proceeded,

"You all must have read about Baba's mast contacts. How these God-intoxicated souls recognized Baba. You see, they recognized in Baba the image of God they revered and worshipped. If the mast was a lover of Krishna, then he saw Baba as Krishna, if the mast was a devotee of Ram, then he saw Baba as Ram. There were others who saw Baba as Allah, Vitthal and so on. Most of these spiritually advanced souls recognized Baba in their own image and not as Meher Baba. They recognized the reality behind the form that we call as Meher Baba. Baba Himself has said that He is not the form that we see. He cloaks the reality with the human form in order to make it tangible for us to see and interact. To see Him as He really is, requires great daring. One should have the courage to long and love Him so intensely that nothing else should matter. Only the intense longing for union with Him can take you to the goal. To a soul whose heart is on fire with that longing, it does not matter by what name he calls his Beloved. The Beloved knows and is ever watchful of such souls who eventually become the Beloved's beloved."

Eruch proceeded to give one more example. "Do you know Krishna Nair? You must have seen him at Meherabad. He would keep night watch for Baba. Once while he was keeping watch, his mind was assailed by disturbing thoughts. He tried his best to get rid of it but the thoughts persisted. You all must have experienced such a state of mind in your life. So you know how disturbing it can be. The more you try, the stronger those thoughts become. The same situation Krishna was in. Suddenly Baba turned to him and asked him, 'What are you thinking?' Krishna told Baba that he was feeling disturbed by unpleasant thoughts. At this, Baba told him, 'But why don't you take My name and those thoughts will go away. Krishna replied, 'Baba I am taking your name but the thoughts still persist.' Baba then asked Krishna to sing the dhun, 'Satchitanand Parmanand Meher Baba Vidyanand' for a few minutes to calm his mind. Krishna did it and sure enough the thoughts vanished. Baba then told Krishna that whenever disturbing thoughts plagued his mind, he should sing the above dhun, (which was composed by Baba Himself). There are many Baba lovers who sing the dhun and say it calms their mind. So don't create controversies in His name and about His name. Just call out from your heart. What matters to the Beloved is the love and longing of His lover behind that call."

THE PRICE OF A MASTER'S SLIPPERS

Nizamuddin Auliya was a Perfect Master of great repute. His reputation was such that whosoever came to His darbar never went away empty handed.

Delhi, in those days, was a small town surrounded by barren land. A poor farmer who had lived his whole life in poverty decided to approach the Master for help. His daughter had grown up and, because of his poverty, he was unable to get his daughter married.

On meeting the Master, he explained his predicament. The master asked the man to stay with Him for two days and whatever offerings His disciples gave him during those two days, He would give to the farmer.

But, it so happened, that during those two days, no offerings were given to the Master. Seeing this, the Master removed His slippers and gave them to the man, instructing him to sell them and get his daughter married with the proceeds.

The man was surprised and wondered how a pair of worn out slippers would solve his financial problem. At best the money obtained from selling them would fetch him a meal. Feeling dejected, he took the slippers and started on his journey home.

It so happened that Amir Khusro, who had worked in the King's darbar as a minister, was returning home that day after leaving the King's service. The King had given him seven camel loads of gold and silver for the service that he had rendered so faithfully over the years. He was traveling with all his wealth when he happened to run into the poor farmer.

Amir Khusro was a great disciple of Nizamuddin Auliya and was on his way to meet his Master. He saw the slippers in the hands of the former and recognized them. He could even smell the fragrance of his Master coming from them. He approached the man and asked him what he was doing with those slippers. The man narrated his plight and expressed his disappointment, wondering how he could get his daughter married by selling the slippers.

On hearing this, Amir Khusro asked, "Will you sell me those slippers?"

The man replied, "Yes, but how much will you pay me for them?"

Amir answered, "My entire retirement wealth, consisting of seven camel loads of gold and silver I will give you for those slippers."

On hearing this, the man fainted. When he regained his senses, he could not believe his good fortune. He remembered the Master's words and thanked Him in his heart. Amir Khusro took the slippers and proceeded to meet his Master.

When he did, he was given a warm welcome. After embracing Amir, the Master asked after his health and made other small talk. Finally, the Master asked whether the King had given him enough wealth for his retirement. To this Amir answered, "Yes, he gave me seven camel loads of gold and silver."

The Master asked, "Where have you kept all this wealth?"

Amir replied, "I gave it to a man in exchange for your slippers."

The Master said, "You have purchased them at a throw away price. The real value of my slippers is much, much, more. They're priceless. You are lucky to get them so cheap."

The Master then turned to His disciples and said, "Amir Khusro loves me so dearly that it is my wish that his grave should be alongside my grave. If you bury him elsewhere, his love is such that he will come out of his grave to be by my side." It is for this reason that Amir Khusro's grave is along side the grave of the Perfect Master, Nizamuddin Auliya.

ESTABLISH THE INNER LINK

"This incident happened at a time when Baba was still talking. When Baba went to Quetta, He stayed at Rusi Pop's place. Rusi Pop happens to be Dr. Goher's father." Mani paused and then continued, "You see, Rusi Pop was a very successful man. He had a grand restaurant and an even grander house. In those days there were no telephones, but they had an internal telephone in their house. It was a communication device for communicating between two rooms and also between the ground and first floor. It looked like a telephone. You picked it up and dialed and the phone rang in the other room.

"It so happened that one day, Baba rang the phone and Gulmai [Adi Sr's mother], who was on the first floor, picked it up. Baba asked Gulmai, 'Can you hear Me?' Gulmai replied, 'Yes, Baba.' Baba then asked, 'Can you see Me?' Gulmai answered, 'No Baba, I can't see You but I can hear You.'

"Baba added, 'Even though you can't see Me, you can hear Me because you are connected to Me through this line. In the same way, no matter how far away you may be from Me, keep your spiritual connection to me by remembering Me, and then you will be able to hear My voice within your heart.' "

Mani concluded, "Just as the telephone line is needed to talk and hear externally, so also the inner link is needed to be able to talk and listen to Baba when He is not physically present."

LOVE FROM A DISTANCE

Pukar was a very close lover of Baba. He longed to live with Baba just as the Mandali did, and often expressed his longing to Baba. Baba would assure Pukar that He would call him at a future date to live with Him permanently. However, Baba did allow Pukar to stay with Him on various occasions. Baba called Pukar His Hanuman. Pukar had accompanied Baba on His tour of South India. Subsequent to that, when Baba was Living at Meherazad, Pukar too was allowed to live with the mandali.

During this period, Pukar saw a side to Baba which He had not experienced before. Baba was very fiery and would often take Mandali to task for no apparent reason. To see Baba treat His Mandali so harshly surprised Pukar. After a period of time, Baba sent Pukar back into the world with the assurance that next time He would call Pukar to live with Him permanently.

Time passed and one fine day, Baba decided that it was time to invite Pukar to join Him permanently. Baba wrote to Pukar to tell him that if he so desired, then he could come and join Baba and live as one of His Mandali, thus fulfilling his longing of so many years. Having seen how harshly Baba treated His Mandali and realizing that serving and pleasing Baba was no easy task, Pukar wrote back saying, "Baba, pyar chahiya magar door se" which, in English, means "Baba, I want your love, but from a distance."

MEHERWAN PINCHES BABA'S EAR

A Baba lover, named Devekey, once asked me if Baba made any sound while laughing. I remembered Eruch telling me that Baba did not make any sound while coughing. Only when Baba was passing wind could one hear the sound of it.

Devekey told me that she attempted it but could not do so — it was impossible to cough without making a sound. She also mentioned that she was able to laugh silently and sneeze silently. She asked me to try and I found that I was also unable to do it. This created a doubt in my mind and I decided to phone Meherwan Jessawala to check out the facts, as all the Mandali had passed away.

Meherwan confirmed that Baba made no sound while coughing. He said that when Baba coughed, there would be much pressure on His face and body that it was difficult to see Him suffer like that. He suffered internally just to maintain His silence for our benefit. Then Meherwan proceeded to tell me the following story: "Sometimes, while gesturing, Baba would make a very faint sound, hmm, hmm, hmm. This he did up until the 50's. After 1959, Baba had me start coming to spend a month each year, around His birthday, to Meherazad. During one of these visits, Baba announced that He wanted to stop making even that small sound. He told everyone present that, in case He slipped, that we should remind Him of it

On the second day, Baba did slip and made the 'hmm, hmm,' sound. I raised my hand and when Baba asked me why, I told Him that He had slipped and made a sound. At this, Baba asked me to come and pinch His ear very hard for having made that mistake. I had to do it but it was so painful for me that, in my heart, I prayed and said 'Baba, please don't put me through this again.' After that incident, Baba never slipped again. He was completely silent after that."

KRISHNA ABSORBS THE BLOW

Eruch would often say that the Avatar does not alter one's destiny, but, if you call out to Him in crisis, He softens the impact of the suffering that would have befallen you, by taking it upon Himself.

The following story reveals how the Avatar takes on the impact of the suffering that would have befallen His lovers. It so happened that during the Mahabharata war, Krishna was Arjuna's charioteer. When Karna and Arjuna were locked in battle, it was not only Krishna's guidance, but also His physical presence that saved Arjuna from disaster, for Karna was a better warrior than Arjuna and Krishna knew it.

During the battle the two warriors would shoot arrows at each other, often neutralizing the opponent's arrow mid-air. Once in a while, an arrow would pass through the opponent's defense. As the charioteer dodged the arrows, some of them would impale upon the chariot. When Karna's arrow would hit Arjuna's chariot, the charior would move back by about a foot due to the force of the impact

At this, Krishna would applaud and say, "Well done, Karna." When Arjunaa's arrow would impale Karna's chariot, Karna's chariot would be pushed back around five feet, but Krishna would make no comment. This went on for some time. Seeing Krishna applaud Karna every time, Arjuna could take it no more. He finally confronted Krishna and said, "Why is it that you applaud Karna and not me, when my arrows knock his chariot back by five feet, whereas his arrows only knocks back by one foot?"

Krishna smiled and said, "I will answer your question, but first I need to relieve myself, so could you ask a charioteer to take my place for some time?" Arjuna agreed and the battle continued with the new charioteer taking over the reins. After some time, one of Karna's arrows impaled Arjuna's chariot and Arjuna was horrified to see that his chariot was forced back 20 feet by the arrow's impact.

Krishna, who had been watching from a distance, came up to Arjuna and said, "Now you understand why I was applauding Karna. The force of his arrows pushed your chariot 20 feet backwards. It was my presence on the chariot that softened the blow and absorbed the impact of his arrows." Krishna added, "Uptil now, I have not come across a warrior who could knock my chariot back by even an inch. Karna is the only warrior who has managed to force it back by a foot and that in itself shows his great strength."

Arjuna realized his mistake. With Krishna's guidance, Arjuna finally manages to kill Karna. Having done that, Krishna asks Arjuna to get off the chariot as He wanted to take the chariot to a remote place and abandon it. Not understanding what Krishna was upto, Arjuna blindly obeys. Krishna takes the chariot a little distance away and then steps down. As soon as Krishna moves away, the chariot explodes into fire and burns down. Walking up to

Arjuna, Krishna smiles and says, "Had it not been for Me, Karna's arrows would have burned your chariot down."

BABA IS EVERYWHERE

"Max Haefliger, a Western Baba lover, had sent us some photographs of the Swiss mountains. We were with Baba at Meherazad when we received those photographs. He wanted to know at exact spot on the mountain Baba had sat during His seclusion work." Mani paused for a while before continuing.

"We, the ladies, were with Baba in dining hall when I decided to show the photographs to Baba. Mentioning Max Haefliger's request, I asked Baba 'Could you point out to me exactly where on the mountain You sat during Your seclusion?'

Baba looked at the photograph with great interest, smiled and put His thumb on the photo, covering the whole mountain and returned it to me. I was surprised by what Baba had done. Thinking He had not understood my question, I asked Him again, 'Baba, Max wants to know the exact spot where You did your seclusion work on the mountain.'

Gesturing to me, Baba said, 'But I already told you.' Baba again put His thumb on the photo, covering the whole mountain and added, 'I was everywhere.' When Baba said this, I realized how petty we are when we restrict Baba to a spot or a particular form. His grace is such that He showers His bounty everywhere He goes. His love flows out in abundance and is not restricted to a certain area."

Another incident Mani narrated which shows Baba's bounty and abundance of love is as follows.

Mani said, "My brother Behram would often send me a box of photographs of Baba which he wanted Baba to touch. Baba would touch all the photographs, which would then be sent to Behram. My brother would send these Baba touched photographs to Baba lovers who wanted them. On one occasion, he sent me a box of photos. This incident happened a few months before Baba dropped His body. I went into Baba's room with the box. Seeing that Baba was not feeling well that day, I decided to put it off for another day. As I turned back, Baba called out to me and asked, 'What is it? What do you want?' I said, 'It's okay, Baba. It can wait another day.' Baba pressed me, 'But what is it? Tell Me.'

"I showed Him the box of photos which Behram wanted Baba to touch. Baba asked me to bring it. He put His hand over the top photo and gestured to me that I could send it to Behram. Now usually Baba would touch every photo, which He hadn't done this time. I asked Baba if it was okay to tell Behram that all the photographs had been touched. With a very serious expression on His face, Baba pointed His finger tip toward the box and said, 'Even if I were to touch my finger tip to the box, not only is everything in the box touched, but also the whole place receives my touch.' While gesturing, Baba pointed the finger tip as if was penetrating the box, coming out from the bottom and pointed towards the ground as it was penetrating the ground and probably coming out from the other end of the universe. Such is His bounty."

GAIMAI JESSAWALA

When I was living at Meherazad, I developed a close bond with Gaimai Jessawala. Gai mumma (mumma means mother in Gujarati) as we affectionately called her, happened to be Eruch Jessawala's mother. Baba had said that she would be His mother in His next advent. I would spend time with her daily and she would share Baba stories with me. If I went away for a few days, she would keep asking as to when I would return. On returning, she would tell me how she missed me.

Gai mumma, along with her family, had lived with Baba from 1938 to 1942. When Baba asked Eruch to quit everything and join Him, He also instructed Eruch to ask his family to dispose of all their worldly belongings and join Him. Gai mumma was overjoyed at receiving the news. She told her family, "People long for the opportunity of being with the Avatar and don't get it. How lucky we are that the Avatar Himself has asked us to be with Him."

One of the duties that Baba gave Gai mumma was to serve His mother, Shireenmai, and obey her at all times. When Shireenmai visited Baba and stayed in the ashram for a few days, Gai mumma would attend to her. She shared a few stories of her interaction with Shireenmai which I now wish to share with you.

Gai mumma said, "Shireenmai was a strong willed woman. Meherwan [Baba] was her favorite child whom she affectionately called Merog. She did not like the fact that He proclaimed Himself to be

God. She had difficulty accepting that He was God and would often plead with Him to return home with her. Occasionally, she would get angry and tell Baba 'Stop pretending that you are God. It is not good that you are allowing people to garland you and bow down to you and embrace you. Stop this hypocrisy and come back.'

"She also did not like the Western women Mandali and often picked on them. However, she liked me and was very nice with me. In India, as you know, many religions have the practice of considering women as unclean and unholy during their period, when they're not allowed to touch anyone or anything. The fact that the Western women Mandali did not follow such practices and touched Baba, annoyed her. She would make sure that a woman having her period did not approach her or touch any of her things.

"Knowing this, Baba once asked me to lie to Shireenmai and tell her that I was having my period. When Shireenmai was resting, she would ask me to press her feet. So, on one occasion, when she asked me to press her feet, as per Baba's order, I said, 'Shireenmai, I am having my period.' She replied, 'It's okay if you touch me, but the others cannot do so. You tell them that if they are having their periods, they should not come near me.' The women Mandali were scared of her because of this, especially the Westerners."

Gai mumma also remembered the time when they had disposed of all their property and went to live with Baba. Shireenmai came to know of this and was very upset as the Jessawala's were rich and influential and Baba made them give up their luxurious life to live in the ashram. Shireenmai met Baba and remarked angrily, "What have you done, Merog? You have ruined their lives completely. God will never forgive you for this."

When certain miraculous incidents happened around Baba, which proved His divinity, Gai mumma would narrate these to Shireenmai and then ask, "Now do you believe He is God?" Shireenmai would stubbornly refuse to accept this, saying, "No. He is not God. That incident which you call a miracle was only a coincidence." It was many years later that Shireenmai finally accepted Baba as God.

Except for Eruch, Baba asked Gai mumma and the rest of the family to move to Poona in December 1942. Reluctantly they left and, from that time till 1990, they lived in Poona at Bindra House. Baba frequently visited them there.

In 1990 Gai mumma had a stroke which debilitated her and from which she never recovered completely. In addition to this, the landlord who owned Bindra House, wanted the premises vacated of all tenants so that he could demolish Bindra House and erect a tall building in its place. Meherwan wrote to Eruch informing him of the situation Eruch wrote back asking Meherwan to shift with the whole family to Meherazad as this appeared to be a call from Baba to leave the world and live with Him in His ashram.

I met Gai mumma for the first time in 1990 when I was visiting Meherazad. Subsequently, when I went to live there I had the good fortune of spending a great deal of time with her. On days when pilgrims visited Meherazad, she enjoyed interacting with them. She would even sit in the Mandali Hall, listening to and enjoying Baba stories. In the evening, about 5 to 5:30, she would take her evening walk. By this I mean that she would take small painful steps on the veranda while Manu and Meherwan supported her on either side.

On one occasion, she was seated with Manu and Meherwan on the veranda when Meherwan commented, "It's time for your evening walk." She was in intense pain that day and told Meherwan that she was in no mood for a walk. When Meherwan kept pressing her, she exploded and said to Meherwan, "If you want to take me for a walk, then you carry me. Otherwise don't trouble me." Manu started laughing at her sudden outburst and commented, "Look at her temper. She explodes suddenly like a bomb." She then embraced Gai mumma and calmed her.

Next day I visited her in her room to inquire about her health. On entering I noticed she was lying in bed, staring at Baba's photo on the wall and complaining. Talking to the photo she said, "Don't you feel ashamed, harassing an old person? Don't you feel any pity?" In order to cheer her up, I said, "Gai mumma, He harasses everyone. Do you know why? Because Shireenmai pampered Him as He was her favorite child. She did not discipline Him and you know a pampered child always ends up troubling everyone. However, we can rectify this situation in the future. Baba said you will be His mother in the next advent. So make sure you discipline Him properly so that He is well behaved and does not cause trouble anymore."

Gai mumma laughed when I said that and then commented, "No one can discipline the Avatar. He is not only mischievous, but also the most slippery one. He takes the advent with the sole purpose of disciplining a wayward world and showing it the path to God."

TO BREAK A PROMISE

Mahatma Gandhi had met Meher Baba on a ship named Rajputana when he was going to attend the round table conference in England to which the British government had invited him. It so happened that the Mayor of Karachi, Mr. Jamshed Metha, who was a Baba lover, impressed upon Gandhiji to meet Meher Baba as Baba was traveling on the same ship to meet His lovers in England.

Gandhiji was not inclined at first, but eventually conceded. The reason behind Gandhiji not wanting to meet Meher Baba was that Baba was Upasni Maharaj's disciple. When Gandhiji first heard of Upasni Maharaj's greatness, he went to meet him and pay his respects. Upon meeting Upasni, Gandhiji introduced himself as Mahatma Gandhi. Upasni got angry and said, "Who says you are a Mahatma?" (Mahatma is a term generally used for advanced spiritual souls on higher planes.) Gandhiji was a great human being and had done great work for the country but he wasn't a spiritually advanced soul, which is why Upasni Maharaj was scolding him or, should I say, abusing him.

Failing to grasp the significance of what Upasni Maharaj was doing, Gandhiji left with disgust. He didn't understand that abuse of a Master is a blessing in disguise. He also could not digest the fact that Upasni Maharaj, who was naked except for a gunny sack covering his groin, was a Perfect Master. When Gandhiji heard that Meher Baba's master was

Upasni Maharaj, he refused to meet Baba initially, but later conceded.

Gandhiji went to Baba's cabin and introduced himself and said, "I have come to meet Meher Baba because Jamshed Mehta asked me to and I have only five minutes to spare for it." Baba welcomed Gandhiji and they talked about various spiritual subjects. Baba made Gandhiji read a chapter from Baba's secret book (which is not yet found to this day). Gandhiji ended up spending more than an hour with Baba. He was so impressed with Baba's writing that he said to Baba, "Baba, what you say is very profound and the whole world should know of it. It should be translated into vernacular languages so that the masses can read it."

Baba said in reply, "Why don't you do it.? Your command of Gujarati is perfect." Gandhiji expressed his helplessness and said, "Baba, I am involved in India's freedom struggle and don't have time for all this." At this, Baba commented, "If I were to give India freedom, do you promise to quit politics, come and join me and do my translation work?" Gandhiji replied, 'If India gets freedom, I promise to quit and join you." Baba stated with all the authority of an Avatar, "I will see to it that India will get its freedom. When that happens, you must quit politics and join me immediately."

When India got its independence, Baba reminded Gandhiji of his promise. Gandhiji expressed his inability to quit politics and come as the country was in turmoil because of the Hindu-Muslim riots and his presence was still required. Baba sent several reminders but Gandhiji was unable to extricate himself from the situation and come to Baba. Baba finally sent one of his Mandali members with a message for Gandhiji telling him that 'Baba has rleased him [Gandhiji] of his promise.'

A few days after the message was conveyed, Gandhiji was assassinated. When the news reached Baba, He said, "Just in time I released him from his promise, otherwise he would have suffered a lot in his next life. To give a promise to the Avatar and not honor it invites a lot of suffering for that soul."

ALOBA'S CHILDLIKE NATURE

I once had to meet a Baba lover who lived in Poona regarding some Trust work. This Baba lover had come into Baba's fold just a few years previously. She had visited Meherabad and Meherazad on several occasions and was close to the women Mandali. When I met her she had a doubt in her mind regarding one particular member of the Mandali, Aloba.

She said, "When you interact with all of Baba's Mandali, they appear intelligent and share profound stories which leave a deep impact on your soul. From their actions they appear to be advanced spiritual souls, except for Aloba. He appears to be the odd one out. He is a little weird in the way he acts. Instead of sharing Baba stories, he catches pilgrims and starts predicting their future. When he talks, he either talks about himself or the tours he undertook in India, the Baba functions he attended, and how he raised money for a Baba Centre. From time to time he also makes a prediction about the third world war and the destruction of three quarters of the world. No other Mandali acts in such a manner. Why is he like that? I can't understand. How can he be one of Baba's Mandali?"

I laughed when she finished. She requested me to ask Arnavaz Dadachanji about this when I meet her as she was close to her. So when I met Arnavaz next, and told her about this, she said, "People fail to understand that where Meher Baba is concerned, it's the heart that matters and not the intellect. Aloba is not intellectual, and he may do things which appear silly to us, but he has a very pure heart. He is like a child, and his love for Baba is child-like, which is, where Baba is concerned, what matters. He does not narrate a story like Eruch or Mani but his faith in Baba is 100 percent. When he makes predictions for pilgrims, he does it with 100 percent faith that it is Baba doing it.

"He often tells pilgrims who approach him with their problems to repeat Baba's name a certain number of times at a particular time during the day and it will solve their problems. Aloba's conviction is such that the pilgrims who followed his advice found that their problems were resolved. It is for this reason many pilgrims flock around Aloba. On a few occasions, when Meherazad was facing a crisis with no apparent solution in sight, Eruch would ask Aloba to read a couplet from Hafiz to see what message Baba had to give regarding the crisis.

"Aloba, with full faith, would put Hafiz's book at Baba's feet in Mandali Hall, recite a prayer and then open the book and read the couplet out. The message would always deal with the crisis and guide us. Aloba's faith is similar to a child who has 100 percent conviction that his parents will take care of him, no matter what the situation. It is for this reason that Baba kept him by His side. When Baba started the Babajan school, Aloba was one of the pupils. When the school was disbanded, he left. Much later he joined Baba again. He even accompanied Baba in the New Life and stayed with Him till the very end.

"A child is not learned and may do silly things but the love of the child is very pure. That's how Aloba is."

BABA IS FIRE

A resident told me the following story. In the early years, when Baba was living at Meherabad, a man had come from Poona for His darshan. This man was not a Baba lover and his sole aim in coming to Baba was to expose Him as a con-man. After taking Baba's darshan, the man pleaded with Baba to bless him with a child, telling Baba that he had no children.

The truth was that the man had three sons and he was trying to trick Baba. If Baba blessed him because of his pleading that he had no children, then he could go and tell the world that Baba was a fraud, for if Baba was God then He should have known that he already had three children.

When the man asked Baba to bless him with a child, Baba became silent. With a look of serious concern on His face, Baba said, "Ask for anything else, but do not ask for this." The man continued pleading, "By God's grace, I have everything I need; the only thing I don't have are children of my own. Please bless me so that I have one child."

Baba warned the man, telling him, "What you are asking from Me might cause you suffering. Be happy with what God has given you and don't ask for a child. Ask for something else and I shall definitely give it to you."

The man was adamant about what he wanted

and insisted, "Baba, I want one child." Finally, Baba said, "Are you absolutely sure that you want one child" The man said, "Yes, Baba" so Baba blessed him saying, "All right, then I bless you and you shall have one child. But don't say that I didn't warn you." The man thanked Baba and left.

When the man went back to Poona he went around telling everyone about what had happened and proclaimed Baba to be a fraud. He went about the task in a vigorous way. It so happened that within a short while, two of his children fell seriously ill. The doctors were unable to diagnose the disease and the children finally succumbed to this strange illness. The man was completely heartbroken and grief stricken. He could not understand why all this had happened. It was only a few days later, when the man was reflecting over the situation that he remembered with horror Baba's warning and now understood its true significance.

Baba had told him not to ask for a child, to be happy with what God had given him and had even warned that it would bring him suffering. It was now clear to him that Baba had known all along that he had three children. By being adamant and insisting that Baba give him one child, he had become the cause of his childrens' death. Baba had blessed him with one child and now he was left with one child only.

Fearing for the safety of his only surviving child, he went running to Baba for His forgiveness. On meeting Baba, he narrated the whole episode and begged His forgiveness. He pleaded with Baba to see that no harm came to his only child. Baba forgave him and said to him, "I warned you about it, but you would not listen. What could I do?" Baba reassured the man that no harm would come to his only child. The men went away and never returned.

This story reminds of a poem composed by Baba:

Baba Is Fire

- Meher Baba

When you feel cold

And sit near the fire

It drives out your cold

And makes you perspire.

When you feel hungry

And cook on the fire,

It gives you your food

For which you aspire.

But if you, like a fool,

Try to play with the fire,

It may burn you so badly

That would make hell admire

.

BABA ENJOYS JOKES

Baba would often ask His Mandali or His close lovers to tell Him a joke in order to lighten the burden of His universal work. At times, Baba would permit them to tell a dirty or adult joke. However, the lover would first have to inform Baba that it was a dirty joke and take His permission before reciting it. If Baba was not in the mood, He would refuse but, more often than not, Baba permitted it.

On one occasion, Baba had invited some Western Baba lovers for His sahavas. Harry Kenmore had also come. He was a blind chiropractor from America who had treated Baba after the car accident in Satara when Baba fractured His hip joint. As Harry could not see Baba because of His blindness, Baba would make him sit near His feet and would pat him from time to time in order to make him feel His presence.

On one occasion, Baba asked Harry Kenmore to tell him a joke. Harry said, "Baba if it is okay with you, can I recite a dirty joke?" Baba gave His consent. A Western Baba lover who was present was shocked and looked at Harry disapprovingly. She felt that Harry had crossed a line with Baba which he should not have done. After all, Baba was God, a divine being that should be worshipped. The idea of Harry telling a dirty joke to God was totally unacceptable to her.

She tried not to listen to the joke by blocking out

the words. But when Harry finished telling it, Baba laughed heartily and gestured, "I liked the joke very much, Harry. Could you repeat it one more time?"

Baba then turned towards the woman who found the very idea of telling an off color joke to Baba to be offensive and said, "I liked this joke a lot. I want you to hear it carefully so that you can share it with your friends. It's a very good joke."

The woman knew that Baba had divined her thoughts and by asking her to listen to the so called dirty joke in God's presence, He was helping her break the conventional idea that she had of God and spirituality.

BABA—THE ETERNAL PERFECT MASTER

Some Baba lovers feel that as Baba is not here in the physical body to guide them, they should go out looking for a living Master. This is a big mistake as Baba is not only the Highest of the High, but He is the eternal Perfect master. Baba, Himself, had stated that "He is available at all times and for all times" and there was no need for His lovers to approach anyone else.

The following story, narrated by Meherwan Jessawala should serve as encouragement for Baba lovers to hold onto Him more tightly.

Chanji was Baba's first secretary. By nature he was very restless and could hardly be still. On one occasion, Baba sent him to Sakori with a message for Upasni Maharaj, one of the five Perfect Masters of the day. After delivering the message, Chanji did not wait but left immediately. Some of Upasni's disciples called out to him as he had forgotten to take Prasad from Upasni.

Chanji, who had left in a hurry, was already some distance away and did not hear them. It is considered that the one who receives Prasad at the hands of Perfect Master receives spiritual blessing so the disciples turned to Maharaj and asked Him if they should go after Chanji and bring him back for the Prasad. Maharaj replied, "He does not need my

Prasad. He has Meher Baba and does not need
anything more."

A PRACTICAL GOD

A Baba lover friend of mine once told me that she had facial hair which embarrassed her, but she could not go to a beauty salon to have it removed because of Baba's instructions.

I was surprised and said, "I don't remember Baba preventing anyone from going to a beauty parlor."

The girl said, "He wants us to live a simple life, isn't it? That means we should avoid make-up and beauty parlors." I laughed and said, "When Baba said that, He was referring to one's thoughts, words and actions. In fact, Baba wanted one to look good and cheerful at all times."

I then shared a story which Mansari would narrate to pilgrims on many occasions. Mansari would say Baba is a very practical God. When the women Mandali members were living with Baba in the ashram, the dress code was very strict in the early years. They had to wear long sleeve blouses which covered their arms all the way down to the wrists. They also had to wear scarves that covered their heads and necks.

As time passed by, Baba relaxed the head scarf rule and also the long sleeve rule. By doing this Baba set into motion an effect that was felt worldwide and later resulted in the so-called women's liberation movement. Baba's every act with the Mandali at that level, had an impact, at a larger level, with the whole world.

When Baba was planning to enter the New Life on Oct. 16, 1949, He called all the women Mandali and took a promise from them that they would obey Him implicitly. He selected Mehera, Mani, Dr. Goher and Meheru to accompany Him on the New Life. Mansari was asked to stay on Meherabad Hill along with Kaikobad Dastur and his family. Everyone else was sent back into the world.

Out of all the women who were being sent away, Baba asked Rano, Kitty & Katie Irani to get jobs. Before they left, Baba called all three of them and said, "Remember, now you all will be living in the world and not in the ashram. So you should wear a proper dress, not the kind you wear in an ashram."

Then Baba made a gesture of rubbing His lips with His finger and rubbed His palm on His cheeks, telling them, "Apply some lipstick and also some make-up to look good." Mansari concluded by saying, "What a practical God He was. He asked them to dress up and apply a modest amount of make-up so as to look presentable when living in the world."

When I told my friend this story, she felt very happy and thanked me for it.

ALL POWERS COME FROM BABA

Amar Singh Saigal had a child-like nature and loved Baba immensely. He was a politician but, unlike other politicians, he was a simple man. He was a member of Parliament. Whenever he got an opportunity, he would talk about Baba with his political colleagues. In fact, he talked only about Baba and because of this, his colleagues would avoid him, for they knew if he cornered them, then he would talk nonstop about Baba for hours.

In the 1960's he heard about the Miracles of Satya Sai Baba. He was fascinated to hear stories of how Satya Sai Baba would remove things from thin air and distribute them as prasad to those who came for darshan.

On one occasion, when he had the opportunity to meet Baba, he broached the subject, saying, "Satya Sai Baba has these miraculous powers, with which he removes things from thin air and gives to his devotees. I too would like to go for his darshan with Your permission." Baba appeared excited at this idea and said, "Yes, that would be a nice thing to do. You go, take darshan and let's see what he gives you. And bring back something for Me."

So Amar Singh Saigal went to meet Satya Sai Baba. He stood in the queue along with all the others. When his turn came, Satya Sai Baba reached out his hand in the air, but nothing appeared. He tried a second time, but still nothing appeared. He tried again for a third time and, when nothing appeared, he turned to Amar Singh Saigal and asked, "Who are You? Where do you come from? And who is your Master?"

When Amir Singh told him that his Master was Avatar Meher Baba, Satya Sai Baba said, "Why have you come to me? Your Master is the Highest of the High, and whatever powers we have comes from Him. Unless He sanctions it, we cannot give anyone anything. So you go back to Him."

Amar Singh narrated the whole incident to Baba and said, "From now on Baba, I won't go to anyone, no matter what miracles they perform."

EVERYTHING ORIGINATES FROM KRISHNA

Lord Krishna would ask His disciples to repeat His name as it was the quickest way to reach liberation. Having doubts, Arjuna once broached this subject with Krishna. He said, "The Vedas say that the path to liberation is a difficult one — where one has to perform regular prayers, recite various mantras daily, perform Havans, perform charity by feeding the poor, feeding the Brahmins and so on. Only one doing all this can expect liberation. So all this that the Vedas say, is it wrong?"

Krishna replied with a knowing smile, "The Vedas are correct in what they say, and so am I?" Arjuna was baffled and asked, "How can that be?" Krishna compassionately replied, "The Vedas, the mantras and the prayers, where do they originate from ? The Source of all is My being. They originate from me. So taking My name is the same as reciting mantras, saying prayers and doing the other duties as prescribed in the Vedas."

BABA REFORMS AN ALCOHOLIC

Adi K. Irani told the following story which happened in the 1920s.

"A man whom I knew very well once came to Baba. He lived in Ahmednagar and was an alcoholic. I knew where he lived and also knew his wife and children. Because of his alcoholic drinking habit, his family would often have to face starvation.

"This man met Baba and, after some time, Baba called me and asked me to give this man ten rupees. I was shocked. I said to myself, 'Does Baba know he is an alcoholic? Why is Baba giving him money? He will spend it on alcohol.' If Baba had given the money to his wife, at least for the next 15 days she would be able to feed the family as ten rupees was a lot of money in those days.

"Anyway, the man goes away but, to my surprise, he comes back the next day. He approaches Baba and, again, Baba asks me to give him ten rupees. I was annoyed, but before I could tell Baba anything, Baba silenced me and gestured to me to do as He said. So I gave the man ten rupees.

"Again, he came back the next day as well and meets Baba. I was irritated when Baba asked me to give him ten rupees. I protested and said, "But Baba . .." but before I could say anything more, Baba quieted me. He looked angrily at me and told me to obey Him. So I gave the man another ten rupees.

"This went on the next day, and the fifth day and the sixth and seventh as well. On the eighth day, the man did not come at his usual time, so I thought he would not come. I was wrong. He did come, but in a different way. His clothes were all torn, he was stinking of alcohol and he had tears in his eyes.

"What had happened was that because of his excessive drinking, his family, friend and relatives finally beat him and threw him out of the house. He was disowned by everyone. At that point he felt it deeply and he later told me 'All my family, friends and relatives disowned me, but Meher Baba continued to shower His love on me, in spite of who I am.'

"So he came to see Baba again. On the way he happened to meet another Baba lover who was also coming to see Baba. They began to talk and the alcoholic told him his story, and of how everyone had turned against him. He said that he felt completely unworthy of Baba's love and that he had nothing he could offer to Baba.

"The other Baba lover said, 'But why don't you give him your weakness — you drinking habit ?. It would make Baba happy.' And so it was that the man came to Baba, stinking of alcohol, and with tears in his eyes he said, 'Today, Baba, I have come to give you something. My drinking habit I give up for your sake.'

"Baba appeared happy and showered the man with lots of love. The man was reformed from that day and lived happily with his wife and children."

Adi concluded, "Only god can achieve such a result. If anyone of us whould have attempted to do what Baba did, the man would probably still be an alcoholic.

HALF TRUTH

The following story was narrated by Meherwan Jessawala. It happened during the Blue Bus tour. Baba had taken His women Mandali, along with a few children of His close disciples, on that tour. They had halted at a dak bungalow for rest in Hassan, about a hundred miles from Bangalore.

Journeys with Baba were always filled with hardships and He undertook them with the sole intent of doing His universal spiritual work. When they disembarked for rest in the dak bungalow, which is a government rest house, the children noticed that it had a lot of tamarind trees and the fruits were all ripe, and many had fallen on the ground.

Meherwan says they saw the tamarind fruit and felt tempted to eat it. Although Baba had told them not to eat sour things because it might give them sore throats, they did not understand the importance of pleasing or displeasing Baba because they were only children.

So Meherwan, Najoo, Sarwar, and Meheru went quietly when no one was around and ate the fruit to their hearts' content. They didn't think they had been noticed but somehow Baba got wind of it and called all the children. They knew they shouldn't have eaten the tamarinds so they decided to say, if Baba asked them, that they had tasted the tamarinds but had spat them out. This was not a complete lie as they had spat out the seeds.

And this is what they did. Except for Sarwar who said she hadn't eaten them at all. Baba asked for a cane and gave them a whack on the hand with it for telling a half truth. Then He asked Sarwar again if she had eaten the fruit. Again she said she hadn't and Baba gave her another whack, and another, until she finally confessed.

Meherwan concluded, "In carrying out Baba's orders, if you spoke a half-truth to outsiders it was okay. But when it came to Baba, you had to speak the whole truth."

TO DEAL WITH AN AGGRESSIVE PERSON

A pilgrim once asked Adi K. Irani, "How should one deal with an aggressive person?" Adi replied, "The best thing to do is to keep quiet and let him have his say. Do not say anything to him or engage him in any conversation. Let him vent his feelings and let him go. Later, when you find him in a better frame of mind, you can tell him the points that you wanted to. If he does not listen then, let it be. It's between him and Baba. Do not try to change him — it's not your job. You have not taken a contract from Baba to change such people."

Adi then told the following story. " There was a well-known poet who once composed a poem. His friend happened to read it and strongly suggested that some of the words were inappropriate and they should be replaced with better words which he suggested. The poet, in order to make his friend happy, carried out the changes. This pleased the friend. When the friend left, the poet replaced the changes with the original words. In this manner, both were happy and harmony was maintained. Otherwise, there would have been unnecessary arguments."

At this a pilgrim told Adi, "But this is dishonesty." Adi replied, "No sir, it is not. It is the motive that makes the act honest or dishonest. If you say something to gain or extract something, if your motive is purely selfish, then it's dishonesty. In our case, the motive of the poet was pure — to maintain harmony and also please his friend."

MOHAMMAD MAST

Mohammad Mast was Baba's favorite mast who lived at Meherabad. He was a fifth plane mast. Baba has explained that fifth plane masts are mental conscious souls who are masters of their minds. They are capable of creating and controlling the thoughts of all gross and subtle conscious souls in creation.

Many pilgrims had the good fortune of interacting with Mohammad. He would often come down with strange illnesses wherein he would give up eating food. He would often comment about it, "When my work is over, I will start eating. I have to do this for my work."

When he was in this state, the residents would keep a continuous watch over him, monitoring his condition round the clock. Residents who volunteered would take the watch in shifts, and the medical staff would explain in detail to them what they should do and how they should handle Mohammad.

On one occasion, after Mohammad had come out of his bout of illness, a resident who was keeping watch had a sudden thought. He went to Padri to ask his opinon on the matter.

Padri was one of Baba's Mandali and had been appointed by Baba as Meherabad's caretaker when Baba went on the New Life. He continued to play this role until he dropped his body. At the time of this incident, Padri was also Mohammad's caretaker.

The resident approached Padri and said, "Padri, I was wondering if Mohammed mast can read my thoughts. I got this feeling when I was doing watch around him that he was reading my thoughts."

Padri replied, "Tell me, when you drive in your car through Ahmednagar, do you notice the garbage and shit that lies on either side of the road in so many places?"

The resident said, "Yes, I notice it." Padri asked, "Do you stop your car and get out to study the contents of the garbage?"

The resident replied, "No, I don't do that. I just drive." Padri persisted, "Is it possible, if you so desired, to stop your car and go inspect the garbage?"

"Yes, I could do it if I so wished," the resident answered. Padri then concluded, "It is the same with Mohammad. He is intoxicated with his love for God. He is drowned in it and is enjoying his blissful state. The thoughts of those around are like garbage to him. Why should he look at it? He can, if he so wishes, but he is so busy enjoying his bliss that he has no time for it."

VISITING HOLY PLACES

A Baba lover friend of mine once phoned me up. She was disturbed and wanted to talk to me. She was married into a Baba lover family and was very happy as her in-laws were totally devoted to Baba and Baba alone. Her mother was also a Baba lover. However her father didn't believe in Baba. It so happened that the festival of Ganesh Chaturtithi was going on. Her father would celebrate it every year and wanted her to attend the ceremony which he was going to hold in the house. She felt attending the prayer ceremony amounted to taking part in a ritual. As Baba didn't want us to indulge in rites or rituals, she was contemplating breaking off all ties with her dad, as he was pressuring her to attend the ceremony.

I questioned her in order to get a clear picture "Does your dad treat you and your mother with love and respect where other things are concerned?" She said, "Yes, he is otherwise a loving person." I further asked her, "Does he respect your love for Baba or does he oppose it ?" She replied "He allows us to worship Baba but he doesn't attend any Baba function."

I expressed surprise and asked her, "I can't understand, if he loves you and respects your love for Baba, then why do you want to break off all ties with him ?" She said, "He wants me to take part in the prayer ceremony of Lord Ganesh which is a ritual ."

I said,"On the subject of rites and rituals Eruch had once commented, 'whatever you do from the heart is not a ritual.' So if your dad is really doing it from the heart, then it is not a ritual. Baba also wanted us to maintain harmony at all costs and be loving towards all. Baba would often tell his lovers not to hurt the heart of anyone for he resided in all hearts. By threatening your dad to break off all ties, you are pressuring your dad to give up his devotion to Lord Ganesh. In addition you will be breaking his heart and creating disharmony."

She appeared flustered and asked, "What should I do ?" I replied, "Attend the ceremony with the intention of pleasing your dad and preserve the love and harmony of the house. While the traditional prayers are being recited you can recite Baba's prayer, for after all Baba did say that Lord Ganesha is only a symbolic representation of the very first Avataric Advent. Did you know that?"

As she didn't know , I proceeded to tell her that Baba had said about Lord Ganesha.

"Ganesh represents that same First Soul when He returned into creation as Avatar. Ganesh is none other but the Ancient One — Adi-Purush; he returned after being beheaded, losing his individual finite mind he gained Universal Infinite Mind. Ganesh became the Son of the Father, Shiva, and thus became the Father of all Sadgurus as Shiva became the Father of all Shiv-Atmas.

Ganesh, because of his mischief and curiosity (the same as the Mischievous Chicken's) seeing his mother naked, which was forbidden, (the same as the fruit in the Garden of Eden) finally undergoes annihilation of the limited mind. (Shiva cuts off Ganesh's head.) When the head is cut off, Ganesh lies dead; the mind is unconscious of creation.

When Shiva places the elephant head on Ganesh, Ganesh becomes Infinitely Conscious of the Infinite Unconsciousness.

Ganesh was the first in creation to become God-Realized, and he is that Same Ancient One Who comes down again and again, age after age as the embodiment of Universal Mind.

Living with an elephant's head resting on his torso symbolizes Ganesh's infinite burden, the suffering and agony of man's unnatural sanskaras which it is his work to wipe out.

He is the favorite one, the One never forgotten, for he bears infinite suffering. Ganesh represents the Goal of life — Infinite Mind.

Meher Baba, *Nothing and Everything*

When I finished the narration, I told her how I myself could not relate to Ganesha – God with elephant head until I read what Baba said on the subject. She then asked, "What about going to temple or holy places? Did Baba not say that we should not go to temples or other holy places?"

I expressed surprise and said to her, "In all my years with the Mandali, I never heard such a thing. Also many Baba lovers, who were priests by profession, would visit the Mandali, and I never saw the Mandali reprimand them on this matter. In fact, after Baba dropped his body, Eruch would take the pilgrims on a tour of historical sites connected with Baba. This also included temples, mosques and some other pilgrimage places which Baba had visited. Eruch and Mani had explained on various occasions that Baba had said that by bowing down at such places, he was charging them up, and all such places over the world, for the benefit of those who would bow down there. As Baba lovers, we have Baba's Samadhi and need not go anywhere else. However, Baba has come in our midst to give the whole creation a spiritual push including those who do not know of him. By Baba's bowing down at various pilgrimage sites, Baba has provided even such souls the benefit of his spiritual push if they bow down with a sincere heart. Baba has made the Mandali recite prayers of all religions on several occasions and he has taken part in it. By doing so, he has charged all the prayers for the benefit of those who don't know of him and recite their own conventional prayers."

She continued with her queries "For those who have already come to Baba, is it not wrong for them to go to temples or other holy places?" I replied "I know of many Baba lovers who have met Baba, and they still go to temples, where they recite Baba's prayers and aarti or sit quietly and remember Baba. In fact, Kitty Davy who was one of Meher Baba's Mandali, loved going to church and continued to do so till the very end. In fact, by doing so she earned the respect of the local Christian community and many of them became attracted to Baba and later became Baba lovers."

I proceeded to tell her the story which Mani had shared on many occasions. Mani said, "Rustom and Sohrab, who are Baba's twin nephews ,once decided to go on a vacation to Udvada which is a place of pilgrimage for Zorastrians. They decided that since they had come to Udvada they might as well visit the fire temple. Inside the fire temple, they had the urge to recite Baba's aarti loudly. Now you see our Zorastrian priests, and many Zorastrians also, when they recite the prayers they say the first word loudly and then they mumble the next 2-3 sentences softly so no one can understand. The twins decided to do the same. So they began the prayer by saying 'O Parvardigar' loudly and then mumbled a few sentences softly. In this manner they recited Baba's prayer without anyone becoming any wiser."

Mani concluded, "When the twins recited the

prayers, all those who were present were blessed for, without being aware, they were indirectly taking part in it." I also pointed out to my friend that Mani's own Navjot ceremony (sacred thread ceremony of Zorastrians) was performed in the Ahmednagar fire temple which Baba permitted as it was Shireen Mai's wish even though Mani protested as she wanted Baba to perform it.

Hearing all this, my friend was comforted. However she had one more doubt. "When Baba gave Sahavas, did he not ask his lovers to proceed home straight and not to go to temples or other holy places?" I replied "Baba's exact words were, 'to proceed home directly and not to go here and there.'" I proceeded to narrate an incident which Eruch had shared in the Mandali hall. "A Baba lover, on hearing Baba's order 'To proceed home straight,' asked Baba if it was ok for him to go to a certain place to attend office work and then proceed home? Baba replied telling him and everyone present 'To go home first and then they were free to go anywhere else.' Baba explained that what he gave to his lovers at Sahavas, he wanted them to take home with them. By going here and there it would be frittered away."

When I finished , the girl breathed a sigh of relief and thanked me.

STATUE OF STONE

Whenever the question, whether it was appropriate for Baba lovers to visit temples, mosques or church, would come up, Eruch would share the following story. In Eruch's own words, "It so happened that after Swami Vivekanad gave the famous Chicago lecture his name and fame spread far and wide. Before that he was not known. He was first recognized in the west as a great spiritual authority before he was recognized in India. Because of his fame he was invited by famous personalities and kings, who sought his company in order to hear a few words of wisdom from such a great soul.

"A King once invited him as a royal guest to stay at his palace for few days and address his subjects. Vivekananda accepted the offer. When he arrived at the palace he was given a royal welcome. The King was personally there to receive him. Assigning one of the servants the task of being Vivekanada's attendant, the King ordered the servant to obey and carry out all orders given by Vivekananda.

"After attending to his daily court duties, the king would spend most of his time in Vivekananda's company asking him questions on spiritual subjects. On one occasion the King happened to ask Vivekananda, 'Swamiji, this is something I fail to understand. Your master, Ramakrishna Paramahansa, was a Perfect Master. He had the experience of God Realisation, yet he worshipped a statue of Kali Being God himself, he continued to worship a statue. One who is aware of everything being illusion, must surely know that there is no God in the statue. It is a stone after all.'.

"Vivekananda didn't make any attempt to answer the King. Instead he turned to his attendant and instructed him to pull down a framed photograph hanging on the wall. It was a photograph of the King's father who had passed away sometime back."

Eruch paused and then said after a while, "You see, in most places we have the custom of making a photo frame of a departed loved one and it's hung on the wall as a sign of respect. So when Vivekananda instructed the attendant to bring down the photograph, he looked surprised but did as asked. The king was baffled and wondered what was going on. Vivekananda then asked his attendant to spit on it. The attendant was shocked and so was the king. The attendant politely refused. The King couldn't contain himself and interjected, 'Swamiji I wish to bring to your notice that the photograph is of my father. By asking the servant to spit on it you are insulting me and my family.'

"Vivekananda replied calmly, 'I can't understand why such an act should be considered as an insult by you. Surely you are intelligent enough to know that the frame is of wood and there is a piece of paper inside. It is just wood and paper after all.' The King protested and said 'but the image on the paper is of my father. When I look at it, the personality of my father comes alive in it.'

"Vivekananda smiled and said to the King ' What you said is absolutely correct. In the same manner that which you call a statue of stone has the image of Kali on it making the statue alive and vibrant with the Divinity.'"

SECTION 2

AN ACCOUNT OF KEKI DESAI'S LIFE WITH BABA

KEKI DESAI COMES TO BABA

The following are a series of stories which Keki Desai told his daughter--my wife, Meher.

Keki Desai was born in Navsari, Gujarat. Although most of his family members had become Baba lovers after hearing of Baba through Sorabji Desai (also known as Soma Desai), Keki refused to accept Baba as God. The reason was that it had been impressed upon him from his earliest years that Prophet Zoroaster was the greatest and there were none greater than Him.

Sorabji Desai would often host Baba during Baba's Navsari visits. Sorabji was a respected citizen of Navsari and Baba stayed at his house. Many of the local citizens came for His darshan. When Keki was fifteen years old, one such darshan was held which was attended by his whole family but Keki did not go.

In those days, Chanji, Baba's secretary, would visit Keki's house whenever he came to Navsari. He would talk for hours about Meher Baba, which Keki's whole family would listen to, with great interest. However, Keki would not take part in these meetings.

Keki's father at that point was working in Lahore (now in Pakistan), while the rest of the family was in Navsari. In 1932 Keki had to leave Navsari for a job in Lahore where he settled down. Every year he would come to Navsari on leave and his elder brother would talk to him about Baba's divinity, but it did not leave an impression on Keki.

In 1938, when Keki came to Navsari on leave, his brother gave him a photo of Meher Baba to keep. From that moment on Keki's heart was awakened to Baba's love, and he started taking an interest in Baba. He started reading books on Baba and it made him realize that Meher Baba and Zoroaster were one and the same 'Ancient One'. It dawned on him that the Avatar is the same 'Ancient One' who comes again and again at different periods in history to help the suffering humanity.

In the year 1940, Keki got married and settled down in Delhi in a place called Kashmiri Gate. His wife, Dhun, was a Baba lover from her early years. She had come into Baba's contact through Kaikobad Dastur, who was one of Baba's Mandali and who also happened to be her maternal uncle. She also had Baba's darshan when He visited Sorabji Desai's house.

Keki used to subscribe for the magazine, Meher Baba Journal in which Chanji would write about the day to day activities of Meher Baba. In the Jan.-1941 issue, Keki came to know that Baba was staying in Jaipur, Rajasthan at that time. As soon as Keki read this, he decided to go to Jaipur for Baba's darshan. He left for Jaipur on 1st Feb 1941. Keki did not know

Baba's whereabouts in Jaipur; all he knew was that Baba would be there for a few days.

On reaching Jaipur in the evening, he asked the waiting room attendant whether he knew the whereabouts of a party accompanying a Bombay Seth (boss). In order to conceal His identity, Baba would call Himself 'Seth'. The attendant revealed that such a party had stayed in the waiting room for a few hours and then had left for the Edward Memorial Rest House, which was located in the city.

Keki went to the rest house only to discover that Baba had stayed there for four to five days but had then left for a place called Khawsji Ka Bagh, which was located on the outskirts of the city on the way to the Amber Fort. Keki was new to Jaipur and did not know his way around, but he was determined not to give up his search, as by now he had completely fallen in love with Baba and was eager to have His darshan.

As Keki was searching for Baba, suddenly he saw Chanji standing by the side of the Blue Bus on the main road, talking to Princess Matchabelli. Keki went up and introduced himself, saying that he had come for Baba's darshan. While he was talking with Chanji, Norina went inside and conveyed the message to Baba. In the meantime, Chanji took Keki to the men Mandali quarters and noted down his Delhi address.

At this time, the Second World War was going on and Baba was in strict seclusion, working with Chatti Baba, the spiritual chargeman of France. Baba sent a message through Norina, saying that He was very pleased that Keki had come, but since He was in seclusion, He was not seeing anyone. Baba asked Keki to return home by the first available train.

That same night, Keki returned to Delhi, feeling very dejected. He regretted all the missed opportunities he had over the years when Baba visited Navsari and he hadn't gone for His darshan. Now, after traveling all the way to Jaipur to take Baba's darshan, Baba had refused to meet him because of His seclusion.

Baba, being the most merciful One and also All-knowing, knew the turmoil in Keki's heart. Keki reached Delhi on the morning of the 2nd and, surprisingly, the next morning, Chanji appeared at Keki's place. Baba had specially sent Chanji to console Keki with the message that it wasn't Chanji but Baba Himself who was visiting them. Chanji spent the whole day with Keki and Dhun, talking about Baba and returned in the night to Jaipur. This was Keki's first darshan, even though he did not get to see Baba physically.

KEKI GIVES UP SMOKING

Keki Desai was a chain smoker. He used to smoke thirty to forty cigarettes a day. In the Zoroastrian religion, cigarette smoking is prohibited because fire is considered sacred. Zoroastrians are basically worshippers of fire and they won't even stamp out a fire with their feet as it's considered a sin to do so. Family and friends tried their level best to make Keki give up smoking but he refused to do so.

On Feb 4th, 1940, Keki was to marry Dhun Desai, who was already a Baba lover from her childhood. Dhun did not like Keki's smoking habit and thought of an idea to make him quit. On the wedding night, she told him that she had written to Baba asking Him two questions: one about herself and one about Keki.

When she mentioned this to Keki, he naturally became curious and asked, "What did you write about me?" Dhun replied, "I asked Baba in the letter whether He approved of Keki's smoking habit." Keki immediately asked, "What was Baba's reply?" Dhun answered, "Baba's reply was that He did not like this habit."

On hearing that Baba disapproved of his smoking, Keki said, "If Baba does not like my smoking, I will give it up from this moment." And he did. He remained true to his word and never again smoked in his life.

This astonished his family and friends. One of his friends, who was a very orthodox Zoroastrian and also disliked Keki's habit of smoking, was very surprised at this turn of events. He asked Keki why he had given up smoking and Keki told him it was because Meher Baba did not like it. This impressed him so much that he became eager to meet Baba, for he wanted to know who this man was for whose sake a chain smoker like Keki had given it up. This friend's name was Keki Nalawala and eventually he and his whole family became staunch Baba lovers.

There was just one problem. Dhun had never written a letter to Baba asking him about Keki's smoking. She had made the whole thing up as a way to get Keki to quit. Years later, during the New Life, Baba once lit a cigarette, took a few puffs and then gave it to Eruch. Keki was also there at the time. Baba looked at Keki with a twinkle in His eye and gestured, "I don't want you to smoke."

Even though Dhun had never told Baba about how she had tricked Keki into quitting, Baba, the all-knowing God, knew what had transpired all along.

STATION MASTER

Baba not only brought Keki into his fold, but also used him for His work at different times. Baba would often ask Keki to make train reservations for Him and the Mandali traveling with Him. Sometimes this was thirty to forty people. Keki was able to do this even during the most difficult periods such as during the Second World War and after the partition of India because of his connections in the railways.

These connections were formed by Baba even before Keki had come into His fold. The following is a story of how Keki met a man who eventually helped him with train reservations. As Keki tells it:

In the year 1938, I was returning from Mathura to Meerut by the Frontier Mail. At Delhi Junction, a passenger came into my compartment and sat on the berth facing me. It was evening time so I started reciting my daily prayers. Being a Parsi, we cover our heads with a cap or a kerchief while saying the prayers which I did. The fellow who sat in front of me kept staring at me. When I finished my prayers he asked me in Gujarati whether I was a Parsi. I replied in the affirmative.

He then inquired about my job, my place of residence, where I was going to and other such things. He also talked about himself and mentioned that he too was a Parsi and that he worked in the railways as the Station Master of Meerut Cantonment. He then told me if I ever needed his help in the future, then I should contact him and he would be glad to help me. I was amused to hear this from a stranger and wondered if I would ever really need his help.

Some time later, this Station Master was transferred to Ghaziabad Junction and, eventually, in 1940, to Delhi. In those days, there was an optical shop called Bombay Optical House in the Chandni Chowk area of Delhi which was a meeting place for Delhi Parsis. I regularly visited this shop and, on one such visit, I ran into the Station Master. Chanji, whenever he visited our place, would also accompany me to the shop and I introduced him to the Station Master. Chanji told Baba about the man.

In September 1942, when Baba and party decided to leave Dehradun and return to Meherabad, He asked me to take the help of my Station Master friend to reserve a full railway coach for Himself and the entire Mandali.

The Second World War was still going on and all the coaches were being used for army movements. By Baba's grace, the station Master was able to reserve a whole coach. The Station Master's name was Dhunijisha Mawalwala. On the 10th of September, Baba came to Delhi. I, along with the Station Master was there on the platform to help with the transfer of Baba and the Mandali's luggage to the reserved coach.

When everything was arranged and settled, I introduced the Station Master to Baba who embraced him and gave him a Baba badge. After reaching Meherabad, Baba sent a telegram blessing Dhun, myself and the Station Master.

During Baba's subsequent visits to Delhi, I would take the help of the same Station Master who would leave his office and personally come with me to ensure that the reservation clerk gave us the reservations as per Baba's requirements.

In 1945 he was transferred to Karachi, but as Baba needed him for His work, he was again transferred back to Delhi at the time of partition   and was also promoted as the Station Superintendent of Delhi. Such was Baba's divine game that a complete stranger ended up serving Him without knowing His divine status and eventually became His lover.

BLUE BUS

In December 1941, Baba decided to dispose of the Blue Bus by means of a lottery. He selected a few of His devotees and informed each one of them, by letter, about it. He asked them to send Rs 100 for a lottery ticket that was to be issued in their name.

Baba mentioned in the letter that in Lord Krishna's time, He had His chariot and, in this modern automobile age, the Blue Bus was His chariot. Keki Desai was one of those who received a letter and he sent Baba Rs 100 as instructed.

It so happened that Keki was the winner of the lottery. Baba picked the slip which had Keki's name on it and the lucky number was 51. Baba informed Keki that he was very fortunate to have won the Blue Bus. However, Baba said there were two conditions which Keki had to observe before he could receive the bus.

The first condition was that the bus should only be for Keki's personal use and the second was that he should never hire it out or use it to make money.

Keki was willing to abide by these conditions but he was reluctant to use Baba's sacred Blue Bus for he felt in his heart that it belonged to Baba alone and He should rightfully possess it. So Keki wrote back to Baba informing Him that the Blue Bus was His and His alone and hence he was offering it back to Baba and he prayed that Baba would accept it.

Baba was greatly pleased with Keki's gesture and sent a loving reply mentioning that He had accepted it as it was given out of love.

The Blue Bus was kept in the show room of Sarosh Motor Works which is located on King's Road, Ahmednagar. Before starting His New Life, Baba got the chassis of the Blue Bus removed and had it installed on a platform of bricks and mortar in Meherazad, converting it into a small cabin. It was in this Blue Bus that Baba sat for His Great Seclusion of 40 days from the 22nd of June to the 21st of July 1949.

KEKI FINALLY MEETS BABA

In 1942 Baba came to Dehradun and stayed there for eight months. Baba stayed with the women Mandali at a place called No. 4 Chander Rd, while the men Mandali were put up at No 25 New Road. Keki Desai visited Dehradun every month for his office work. While he was there in April, he came to know from his friend, Keki Nalawala, that Baba was staying in Dehradun. As Keki was close to Chanji, he requested Chanji to help him have Beloved Baba's darshan

Baba was on a mast tour at that time. When Baba returned, Chanji asked Him to give darshan to Keki and two of his friends, to which Baba agreed on the condition that darshan be for only one second.

Keki Desai says that they were told not to fold their hands or garland Baba. They were also not allowed to bow down. Keki Desai's two friends were Keki Nalawala and Adi Noras, both from his native place, Navsari.

Baba told them to come on April 14, at exactly 2 p.m., to No. 25 New Rd. When they entered Baba's room, they found Baba sitting cross legged in a corner with Jal Kerawala near Him. The darshan lasted just for a second. Keki was extremely excited on seeing Baba, but since the darshan was only for a second he could not have a proper look at Baba's physical form.

He felt discontented as he was hoping to have a proper look at Baba's form to his heart's content. He basically wanted to be able to appreciate Baba's beautiful body from head to toe by staring at Him and soaking in His divine beauty.

After this darshan, Keki was planning to go with his wife, Dhun, to Mussoorie which is a hill station located twenty miles from Dehradun. Chanji had informed Baba about Keki's plan. In the meantime, Keki had left for Delhi to pick up Dhun for their proposed visit to Mussoorie. Baba sent a message through Chanji asking Dhun to come and stay for a day with the women Mandali on her return from Mussoorie.

Initially, Baba had arranged that Chanji should go and fetch her on their return to Dehradun. However, later on, Baba altered the plan and asked Keki Desai to bring his wife to the place where the women Mandali were residing. As instructed by Baba, Keki brought Dhun on the 20th of April. Masiji was on guard duty at the bungalow gate. Dhun was taken inside and Baba sent a message for Keki to wait outside.

Baba was seated in the bungalow garden in an armchair and after a few minutes He called Keki. Keki was delighted to finally have Baba's darshan to his heart's content. After some time, Baba asked Keki, "Not that you have seen Me from head to toe, are you satisfied?" Keki replied in the affirmative. Baba knew the thoughts going through Keki's mind and also the longing of his heart and He responded to it.

BABA BLESSES DHUN

Baba left Dehradun for Meherabad on September 10th 1942. He planned to travel via Delhi and He sent Papa Jessawala in advance to Delhi with a message to Keki to reserve a full coach for the Mandali and Himself. Keki took the Station Master, Dhanjishah's help. Baba had told Papa to assist Keki with all the necessary arrangements for the journey. He told Keki to ask Dhun to prepare food for Him and all the Mandali and to bring it to the Delhi train station.

Keki did as instructed by Baba and went to the station, along with Dhun who also had her neighbor's child with her. This child, Suniti, was very attached to Dhun and Keki and would spend the whole day at their place. For all practical purposes, Dhun treated her as her own daughter and attended to her daily needs. Suniti would also tell people that Dhun and Keki were her real parents. Such was the bond between Suniti and Dhun that she decided to take her along for Baba's darshan.

Although Baba is All-knowing, on seeing Suniti, He asked Dhun, "Is that your daughter?" Dhun said, "No Baba, I don't have any children. This child belongs to my neighbor." Baba then asked Dhun, "Do you want a child of your own?" Dhun replied "Not just now, Baba." Baba then said, "Whenever you feel like having a child, think of Me, take My name, and I will give you a baby whom you should name Meher, whether it's a boy or a girl." After this, Baba placed His hand on Dhun's head and blessed her.

Years later, in 1951, Keki and Dhun when they were in Mumbai, visited their relative Minoo Desai, and happened to see his small daughter, Meher. On seeing her, Dhun suddenly felt in her heart a longing to have a baby girl of her own. She remembered Baba's blessings and prayed to Him for a baby. Soon after this, Baba called Keki to Meherabad for some work. On seeing Keki, Baba made a gesture of a small baby and asked him something which Keki could not understand. Baba then took a rose, plucked some petals from it and made Keki eat them.

When Keki returned to Delhi and reported this whole incident to Dhun, she immediately understood what Baba was trying to convey — that He had blessed them and they would have a baby. Soon after this, she conceived.

A year later Dhun delivered a baby girl, on May 19, whom they named Meher. Baba sent Eruch and Pendu with a gift for the baby which they delivered to her in the hospital. In November of 1952, Baba visited Delhi to give darshan. The darshan was to be on the 1st to 3rd of December and Baba arrived on the 29th of November.

Keki went to receive Him. Baba asked about the

baby and told Keki that he would come the next day to see and play with the baby. On previous occasions, Baba always stayed with the Mandali at Keki's place, but this time His stay had been arranged at Mr. W.D. Kain's house. As promised, Baba came to Keki's house the next day. He put the baby on His lap and played with her by tickling her all over the body. Baba stayed the whole day with the family, having His meals there as well.

BABA VISITS KEKI'S HOUSE

On the 1st of 1943, Baba left Meherabad for Lahore (which is now in Pakistan). As Baba's train would be passing through Delhi on the 5th, He sent Keki and Dhun a telegram asking them to bring meals for Him and all the Mandali. He would be traveling on the Punjab Mail.

As Keki was out of town, Dhun managed everything on her own and took the food to the station as per Baba's instructions. Baba then left for Lahore where He stayed for five months. During this period, Baba would often send Chanji for His work from Lahore to Delhi. Chanji would stay at Keki's house when he came. Keki asked Chanji to arrange for Baba to stay at their house when He visited Delhi. Chanji agreed to broach the subject with Baba.

When the time came for Baba to leave Lahore, He sent a letter to Keki explaining to him the arrangements He wanted Keki to make. On the 21st of November, Baba wanted Keki to reserve tickets for the men Mandali, along with Chatti Baba(mast)who would be accompanying them, on the Punjab Mail for Meherabad. Baba wanted a second set of reservations for the women Mandali by the Delhi-Bombay Express from Delhi to Chittorgarh via Ratlam on the 22nd.

On the 22nd the men Mandali, along with Chatti Baba, arrived and Keki went to the station to meet them which gave him the opportunity to see Chatti Baba. Baba was due to arrive the next day at 6:30 am and He had told Keki that He would visit his house for a few hours to rest. Baba gave special instructions to Keki that, apart from Dhun and himself, no one should know about Baba's arrival. He warned Keki that if anyone else came to know of His visit, then He would leave immediately.

Keki went to the station to receive Baba, Chanji and the women. On arriving at Keki's place, they had breakfast. After breakfast, Baba asked Dhun to accompany Him and the women for a visit to the Qutub Minar (a famous historical tower in Delhi). Baba went to the first storey while the women went to the very top. On returning, they had lunch at Keki's place. Baba's train was to leave at 4 pm. So Dhun prepared some meals for the evening and packed it in a tiffin carrier. Unfortunately this tiffin carrier got lost at the Ratlam Station while they were changing trains. This was Baba's first visit to Keki and Dhun's house.

BABA GIVES JUDGMENT

Keki and Dhun had a Nepali maid working at their place. She had three sons. Her eldest son was working in a pharmaceutical company. He was accused of committing a robbery and was jailed because of it. The maid came crying to Keki requesting him to plead with Baba for her son. She was convinced of Baba's divinity and felt that Baba could get her son released from prison through His divine intervention.

When this incident happened, Baba happened to be living at Keki's Desai's place along with the Mandali. Baba said that He would hear the matter out the next day and decide about it. The next day, after having His bath, Baba called the maid. He sat on a small stool with Keki and the maid to His left and Chanji to His right. It was like a court room. After hearing the matter out, Baba gave His judgment. He said that it would be better for her son to undergo a term in prison because if Baba were to get him released, it would not be in the best interest of the maid. So, following Baba's decision, they didn't contest their son's imprisonment which was to last for a few years.

At that time, no one understood what Baba meant when He said that if the son was released from prison it would not be good for the maid. A few months later, the maid, who had been a widow for several years, gave birth to a son. No one knew about her pregnancy or, for that matter, about her affair with someone. She had kept it a secret. Only Baba knew this. Her eldest son, who was in prison, was a very aggressive and violent man. Had he been out of prison, he would surely have killed his mother, the maid, for he was known to be a terror among the locals.

When people came to know of the maid's pregnancy and her son's violent nature, they realized the significance of Baba's words. By allowing the son to go to prison, he not only saved the maid's life, but also prevented the son from committing a heinous crime.

Several years later, when the son was released from prison, he had mellowed completely and did not take any drastic step against his mother. Thus in the so-called act of cruelty on Baba's part was hidden Baba's mercy and compassion.

BABA STAYS AT KEKI'S PLACE

In 1944, Baba sent a telegram from Nagpur to Keki Desai informing him that He would be coming, with His Mandali, to Delhi and that during this period He would stay at Keki and Dhun's house. Baba also asked Keki to get His and the Mandali's reservations on the Frontier Mail from Delhi to Rawalpindi (now in Pakistan).

Before coming to Delhi, Baba had been in seclusion in a hut on top of Angirashi hill in the Raipur District. During this seclusion, He did some very important spiritual work. As soon as this seclusion work was completed, Baba left Nagpur by the Grand Trunk Express for Delhi. He reached Delhi on 14th August 1944.

Keki went to the station and met Baba, Chanji and the women and brought them home. The men Mandali were told by Baba to stay at the Regal Hotel, which is located opposite the Delhi main junction station.

On arriving at Keki's place, Baba had a bath and washed His hair as well. For this He needed four to five buckets of water. Chanji explained that whenever Baba sat in seclusion for His spiritual work, on completion He always washed His hair to lighten His burden.

When Baba finished His bath, He expressed His

wish to contact masts in Delhi. He asked Keki whether he had a suit which Baba could wear to go for mast work. Keki showed Baba his collection and Baba selected a white suit which He wore with white tennis shoes that had been sent for Him by a Western Baba lover. After getting dressed, Baba asked Keki, 'How do I look?" Keki replied, 'Baba, you look like an Englishman."

Baba contacted several masts in Delhi. One of them was the spiritual chargeman of Delhi who lived in Old Sabji Mandi and was known as Naqab Posh Baba. He was called this because he used to cover his face with a veil.

After the mast contacts, Baba returned to Keki's house and Baba's sister, Mani, expressed a wish to see a movie to which Baba readily agreed. In fact, it was Baba who really wanted to go to the theater for His spiritual work which He often did in a crowd where everyone was focused on something, like at a movie, or the circus or a cricket match. It made His work easier when the crowd was absorbed in something. It was because of this that Baba prompted Mani to ask to see a movie. The film Mani selected was "Lassie Came Home," which was the story of a dog named Lassie.

The movie was showing at the Odeon Cinema in New Delhi and Baba sent Keki to purchase tickets for the noon show. Baba, along with the Ladies, Chanji,

Keki and Dhun, went to see the movie. As was Baba's habit, He left halfway through the movie, along with everyone else accompanying Him. Baba almost never sat through an entire movie; He would leave as soon as His work was over. Mani would often say, "With Baba we went everywhere, saw everything, but enjoyed nothing." Wherever Baba went, it was for His work. As soon as His work was over, He would leave immediately.

After returning from the movie, Baba went to contact more masts that evening. By the time Baba finished His mast work, it was late at night and, at exactly midnight, Baba sent a telegram to Ahmednagar from the Delhi General Post office.

The next day, on the 15th, Baba asked Keki to accompany Him to the hotel where the men Mandali were staying. Baba informed Keki that He wanted to give him money for the expenses Keki had incurred in making the reservations etc. Keki protested and said to Baba that everything belonged to Him. Seeing Keki hesitate to accept money, Baba wrote on a bag with His index finger two words — "Prasad," and "Barkat." Prasad is a divine gift and Barkat means prosperity. Baba gestured to Keki and said the money was His prasad and it would bring prosperity. Baba then proceeded to the hotel with Keki accompanying him.

Keki held the umbrella over Baba's head as they

walked towards the hotel. On the way, Keki mentioned to Baba that, in spite of being in Baba's contact, he often got bad thoughts. Baba told Keki not to worry and whenever such thoughts came, He should take Baba's name and think of Him and this would protect Him.

On the way, they passed a cinema hall called "Novelty." Baba pointed towards it and asked what it was. Keki informed Baba that it was a cinema hall. At this Baba commented, "The whole world is a cinema hall and I hold its key."

When they got to the hotel, Baba took Rs 2,000 from Kaka Baria, who looked after the accounts, and gave it to Keki as His Prasad. Baba then asked Keki to go back home alone. Baba returned much later with Baidul.

That same night Baba left for Rawalpindi by the Frontier Mail. Before leaving for the station Baba did a very strange thing. He made Dhun and Keki embrace Chanji several times. Although they were very close to Chanji, they would usually embrace him once before departure and so they could not understand why Baba asked them to embrace Chanji again and again.

Sometime after Baba left, the news of Chanji's passing away appeared in the Parsi newspaper. On reading this, Dhun and Keki understood why Baba had made them embrace Chanji several times. Baba knew this would be their last meeting. For after leaving Delhi, Baba had gone to Rawalpindi and from there to Srinagar where Chanji passed away, to live eternally in His Beloved, Meher Baba

BABA CREATES A PROTECTIVE SHIELD

In the last week of September 1944, Baba sent Baidul to Delhi. Baba also informed Keki to accompany Baidul to Agra and look for a suitable accommodation for Him and the Mandali as He wished to stay there for a few days in October.

The Second World War was still going on and, Agra being an American Air Force base, all the bungalows were occupied by the American air force officers. Baidul and Keki, despite this, somehow managed to find an accommodation in a hotel named the Agra Hotel with was situated in the army cantonment area. The hotel staff agreed to make the necessary alterations to suit Baba's needs, as Baba was very particular that the ladies accompanying Him should have their privacy and not be disturbed by anyone. Baidul stayed in Agra and Keki returned alone to Delhi.

Soon afterwards, Baba telegrammed Keki informing him that he would be passing through Delhi on the 30th of September by the Peshawar Express and asked Keki to meet him at the station. Keki met Baba and gave him a report about the accommodation arrangements, after which Baba proceeded to Agra.

On the 2nd of October Keki received another telegram from Baba in which He mentioned that he was coming to Delhi on the 3rd and asked Keki to be in readiness to accompany Him to Sonepat, Panipat and Meerut for His mast work. Baba came with Baidul on the third evening by the Punjab Mail and Keki received him at the station and brought them home. This was Baba's third visit to Keki's house.

After dinner, Baba asked Keki to accompany Him for a walk. They went by the main road and on reaching the road's end, known as Mori Gate, Baba stood for some time and surveyed the surroundings. After a few minutes, Baba decided to return, but He did not want to go back by the main road. He wanted to return through the smaller by-lanes. As these by-lanes were crowded and dirty, Keki repeatedly requested Baba to go by the main road. Baba, however, insisted on walking through the narrow by-lanes which they did.

Keki could not understand the significance behind Baba's act at that time. However, two years later, in 1946, Hindu-Muslim riots broke out in Delhi and there was a great massacre everywhere. The building in which Keki Lived, Hasan Building, was owned by a Muslim and the by-lanes through which Baba had walked had a major Muslim population living there. Surprisingly, during the riots not a single person in that area was killed and not a single building was burned.

In fact, a mob had come to burn down Hasan

Building and everyone had fled their homes beforehand and had gone to some safer places. Dhun was living alone as Keki was on a work tour, and she refused to leave because she had full faith in Baba. When the neighbors pressurized her to leave the place, she told them that Baba was always with her. Also that Baba had stayed at their place often, therefore no harm would come to the building. Strangely enough, her prediction came true and the mob, for some reason, left without burning the building.

A similar incident happened in 1984 after Indira Gandhi had been assassinated. All over Delhi, Sikhs were being massacred because the person who had killed Indira was a Sikh. During this time, the area surrounding Keki's placed consisted of commercial shops which were predominantly owned by Sikhs. Surprisingly, this time too, not a single shop was burned nor a single person killed in the area. Baba, in order to protect His lovers, had created a protective shield over the whole area by walking through the by-lanes on the way to Keki and Dhun's home. This kept their building and all of the nearby residents safe through two different riots.

After the incident where Baba had done this, He left Delhi on the 4th of October. He changed His previous plan of going to Sonepat, Panipat and Meerut and instead decided to go to Mathura. Baba, along with Baidul and Keki, traveled by train to

Mathura where He contacted masts, including the spiritual chargeman of Mathura whose name was Inayat.

While returning, it started raining heavily and all three got wet. On reaching the railway station waiting room, Baba removed His wet coat, sadra and pajama. Since Baba was not carrying any spare clothing with Him, He asked Keki to give Him a spare Pajama if he had one. Keki had an extra pajama which he gave to Baba who wore it. They then slept on the floor of the waiting room, side by side. The next morning, Baba returned Keki's pajama to him and asked him to go back to Delhi. Baba and Baidul left for Agra.

HOW BABA REMOVES SANSKARAS

Baba decided to leave Agra on the 7th of October, 1944 and return to Meherabad. Baba instructed Keki to get train reservations on the Punjab Mail for Himself and the Mandali. They would be boarding the train at the Agra Cantonment, however, the reservations were to be made from Delhi to Manmad.

Baba gave specific instructions to Keki to see that an entire coach was reserved and that no one was to be allowed in the coach from Delhi to Agra. Keki was to travel all by himself in that coach and come to Agra. So, as per Baba's instructions, Keki reserved a complete coach and when he got inside, he pulled down all the window shutters and locked the door from inside so that no one else could enter.

The journey went smoothly until Mathura. However, as the train was about to leave, someone started knocking incessantly on the compartment door. As the knocking did not stop, Keki finally pulled up the window shutter and saw the railway guard with three American tourists. As the train was fully packed, the three Americans who were going to Agra could not get any place to sit so they had approached the guard for help. The guard saw the reservation chart and noticed that one compartment, which Keki was traveling, was going empty. So he asked Keki to allow the three Americans to enter.

Keki refused at first but as they pleaded with him, Keki finally allowed them in, thus breaking Baba's order. When the train reached Agra, the three Americans got down, followed by Keki. To his surprise, Baba was standing right in front of the compartment.

On seeing the Americans get down, Baba got angry with Keki and scolded him for breaking His order. Baba asked Keki to go away and leave Him alone. Keki was upset and broken hearted. He went and sat in the waiting room and wept bitterly. It was the first time that Baba had scolded him.

In the meantime, Baba was served a meal in the compartment. Baba had instructed Keki as part of his orders to make arrangements with the dining car manager at Delhi that as soon as the train reached Agra, Baba should be served His meal in His compartment.

Baba was served vegetable soup along with His meal. Baba drank half the soup and the remaining half He asked Vishnu to give to Keki to drink, which he did. When the time came for the train to depart, Baba called Keki and embraced him. After seeing Baba off, Keki returned to Delhi. Keki kept wondering about the whole incident which had upset Baba.

A few days later, Keki received a letter from

Baba. This letter was dictated by Baba to Kaka Baria while traveling in the train from Agra. In it Baba mentioned that usually He never got angry. On rare occasions when He did get angry with someone, it was with the intention of removing that person's past bad sanskaras. As Keki had now come in His fold and was His, Baba had resorted to this method to get rid of Keki's past bad sanskaras. In fact, Baba said that He was very pleased with all the work that Keki had done for him.

After reading this letter, Keki's spirits lifted once more, for not only was Baba pleased with him, but also considered Keki to be His.

YOU ARE MINE

In December of 1942, Baba called Keki and
Dhun to Ahmedngar to attend Nariman and Arnavaz
Dadachanji's wedding. As Dhun was unable to go,
only Keki went. All the invitees were accommodated
at the Ahmedngar Parsi Dharamshala, which adjoins
the Parsi Fire Temple where the wedding took place.
For four days, from the 18th to the 21st of December,
everyone enjoyed a feast. On the 22nd, everyone was
shifted to Meherabad in order to enable them to
attend the functions which took place there.

During the Meherabad stay, Baba gave Keki a
private audience in His small interview cabin. Adi Sr
was present. It was then that it was revealed to Keki
that Baba had sent a letter asking both Keki and Dhun
to leave Delhi forever and settle down in Ahmedngar
or Bombay, whichever place they liked. Baba had
even sent a money order to Dhun for the train fare.

As Keki had been out of town at the time, he
didn't know anything about the letter or the money
order. Dhun, without consulting him, had replied to
Baba expressing her inability to do so. When Keki
came to know about this, he broke down and wept.
Baba patted him and asked Keki why he was
weeping. When Keki said that he hadn't known of
Baba's wish for them to move, Baba dictated on His
alphabet board the word "Maro" which means
"mine" in Gujarati

At first, Keki could not understand what Baba was saying so Baba repeated His message very slowly, "You are mine." Baba comforted Keki and told him not to worry.

The next day, on the 23rd, Baba's younger brother Adi Jr's first wife was taken to the hospital to deliver her child. Her condition became serious during the delivery and she needed a blood transfusion. Baba sent Keki and a few others who had come for the function to donate blood. Unfortunately, in spite of the doctors' best efforts, she passed away after giving birth to a son, Dara.

When Baba received the news, He took the whole incident lightly and continued with the program as if nothing had happened. On the 24th, Baba held a special function which was attended by all the invitees. A pit was dug next to Masaji's grave in which Chanji's bedding roll was lowered. As mentioned earlier, Chanji had passed away in Srinagar where his body was buried in August of that year.

Baba then had Adi Sr read out from a list the names of all His close ones who had departed and, at the mention of each name, Baba took a rose petal and dropped it into Chanji's grave. During this ceremony, Baba declared that He would come after 700 years.

On the 25th, Mehera's birthday was celebrated.

The next day everyone was blessed by Baba and were asked to return home.

HOW BABA WORKS BEHIND THE CURTAIN

On November 19, 1946, Keki received a telegram and then a detailed letter from Baba. In the letter, Baba instructed Keki to get train reservations for Himself and eleven of his female Mandali on the Peshawar Express from Delhi to Meherabad for the 30th of that month.

He also asked Keki to bring five kilograms of Indian snacks called 'sev gathia' and 'bhajias'. Baba's telegram contained the following message: "Half luggage will go in our compartment and half MUST GO in break van of the same express train." Even though Baba had emphasized MUST GO by writing them in bold letters, Keki did not pay much attention to it as he did not realize its importance.

Baba came, as planned on the 30th at around 2 p.m. by a chartered bus from Dehradun. Baba, with the women, went to Keki's house whereas the men Mandali were sent straight to the Delhi Main Station with the luggage, except for Vishnu Master who was with Baba.

Keki reported that the tickets had been purchased, but the clerk on duty was not giving any assurance that half the luggage would go in the break van of the same express train. The reason was that this train was coming from Peshawar and only on its arrival would the clerk be able to check whether there was any room for the luggage in the break van.

When Baba heard this, He ordered Vishnu to contact the railway luggage clerk on duty and tell him that half the luggage must go in the break van of the same express train. (The other half was to go in their reserved compartment and no permission was required for this as they had reservations.)

Baba stressed several times that the luggage must go in the breakvan of the train. Vishnu went to the station and conveyed Baba's message to the clerk as strongly as he could. The clerk expressed his inability to make any commitment for the same reasons as before.

Baba was taking rest after having lunch at Keki's place when Vishnu returned and reported the matter. After some time, Baba sent him again with the same message as before. When Vishnu went the second time, a new luggage clerk was on duty. This clerk also refused to give any sort of assurance. Vishnu, on returning, informed Baba about this.

After a while, Baba sent Vishnu for a third time, telling him that He would now turn the key. This time, surprisingly, the clerk agreed to take half the luggage in the breakvan as Baba had requested. When Vishnu told Baba this, He was very happy and said, " Shabash!" which means well done.

During this time, there was a curfew in Delhi

because of Hindu-Muslim riots. The curfew was from 8 p.m. to 6 a.m. and lasted for several days. However, on the day Baba arrived, the curfew timings were relaxed to 11 p.m. to 6 a.m. Baba's train was to depart at 10 p.m. and Keki asked Baba if he could see Him off at the station. Baba was worried about the curfew, but when Keki informed Baba about the curfew's hours being changed, Baba agreed and allowed Keki to accompany Him to the station.

After dinner, Baba and party left for the station. On getting there, Baba asked Keki to bring the evening newspaper. When Keki purchased it and brought it to Baba, He asked him to read the headlines. In bold letters the following news was printed on the front page, "Jinnah agrees to go with Nehru in the same plane." Baba then took the newspaper with Him and asked Keki to return home.

The next day, when Keki read the morning newspapers in detail, he understood the significance of Baba's strange actions. The newspaper revealed that Jinnah and Nehru were both invited to attend the Round Table Conference in London by the British government. At that time, there were only two main political parties in India — the Congress and the Muslim League. Nehru wanted Jinnah to go with him in the same plane as he felt that if they traveled together, it would create an impression of unity on the British government which would be good for them.

Jinnah, however, wanted to travel separately. While Vishnu was pleading with the luggage clerk to take half the luggage in the break van of the same express train that Baba would be traveling on, Nehru was pleading with Jinnah to travel in the same plane. Here the clerk was refusing and there Jinnah was refusing. When Baba turned the key and the clerk agreed, Jinnah too agreed at that same time.

Jinnah and Nehru left for London on the night of the 30th and Baba left too for Meherabad that same night. This is how Baba works behind the curtain through His Mandali. All His action, no matter how ordinary they appear, have deeper significance with regard to His work, which He does for the universe.

BABA WATCHES A CRICKET MATCH

Keki received a telegram from Baba in October of 1948. There was also a detailed letter but, although Keki got the telegram, he did not receive the letter. When Keki informed Baba that he had not received the letter, Baba made Eruch write another one. In it, Baba mentioned that He was coming to Delhi on the 10th of November to see the India versus West Indies cricket match and He asked Keki to book tickets

Baba and the Mandali came from Junagadh (in Gujarat) by the Delhi mail on the tenth at 6:30 am. Baba had just completed His seclusion work on Girnar Hill (in Gujarat) and, after finishing His work, He came to Delhi to relax. As usual, Keki went to the station to receive Baba and the Mandali and brought them to his home.

Baba was accompanied by Gustadji, Eruch, Baidul, Vishnu and Chaggan. On this trip too, Baba had a full bath and washed His hair with four or five buckets of water. This is something He usually did after completing seclusion work. Baba came out after having His bath and stood with His hands on His waist with His hair loose and flowing. At that moment, when Keki looked at Baba he saw Baba in the form of Lord Shankar. On this trip since the women Mandali were not there, Baba asked Dhun to comb His hair, which she did.

Baba stayed at their house for four days from the 10th to 14th . One day, during this time, while everyone was having morning tea, Baba suddenly picked up the tea cozy and put it on Gustadji's head. He then asked Keki how Gustadji looked. Keki replied, "Gustadji looks like a Tibetan Lama." Gustadji, with his long Parsi style coat and tea cozy on his head, did indeed look like a Tibetan Lama.

Four years later, in 1952, Tibet was overrun by the Chinese and all the Tibetan Lamas were driven out of Tibet. It was felt by all who were present at that time that when Baba put the tea cozy on Gustaji's head, He was doing His inner work on Tibet, which resulted in the invasion by China and the Tibetan Lamas being driven out.

During Baba's stay, all except Baidul, would daily go to Feroz Shah Kotla stadium to watch the cricket match. Baidul had been instructed by Baba to find suitable masts in Delhi whom He could contact at a later date. When Baba was watching the match, Jawaharlal Nehru, the Prime Minister of India, was also there watching the match, a short distance from where Baba was seated. Nehru started pacing to and fro. It was as if Baba was watching Nehru.

Years later, when Nehru passed away, Baba commented that Nehru was a true karma yogi and that a soul like him would only come during the next Avataric advent after 700 years.

BABA RELEASES THE GHOSTS

The building in which Keki and Dhun lived, known as Hasan Building, was known to be haunted. It so happened at the time of the construction of the building, two workers had fallen from the top and died. It was believed that they had committed suicide and their spirits now haunted the building. Strange noises would be heard, along with strange occurrences which could not be explained. As soon as Keki would receive a telegram or letter from Baba that He was coming, these strange happenings would increase as the ghosts became very active.

In the year 1946, when Baba was at Keki's house, Keki jokingly told Baba that Dhun believed that the building was haunted and she was scared. Keki did not believe that the building was haunted and so he mentioned this to Baba. Baba then informed Keki that it was true that the building was haunted and there were two ghosts and not one. Baba added these ghosts were seeking mukti, i.e., release from their ghost state so they could acquire a human body. This they could achieve if they managed to touch Baba. (It was for this reason that Baba had a Mandali member keep watch near Him while He rested, so that the ghosts would not come and touch His body. On rare occasions when there was no one around for brief periods to do night watch, Baba would keep moving His big toe constantly to keep the ghosts away.)

However, Baba added, as their time had not come, Baba just ignored them. Baba said that He would release them at the appropriate time and they should not feel scared of the ghosts as they would never be able to come inside the house. After this assurance from Baba, Dhun stopped worrying about the ghosts and got used to the strange happenings.

In 1948, when Baba visited again for four days, from the 10th to 14th of November, He said that the time had come to release the ghosts. Baba, as usual, slept in His own room with Eruch keeping night watch. Baba instructed Dhun, Keki and Dhun's cousin, name Burjor Gai, who was at that time living with them, to sleep in the other bedroom and locked the bedroom from the outside. He told the three of them not to get up in the middle of the night no matter what happened. They were told to get up in the morning only after they heard His clap outside their bedroom.

Baidul, Vishnu, Gustadji and Chaggan were asked by Baba to sleep outside the house in the passage where the servants slept. Baba then closed the main door of the house Himself. He also got all the ventilation, door and windows of the bedroom in which He normally slept covered. That night, November 12th, Baba stayed awake and did His work and the next morning He informed all that the ghosts had been released. From that day onwards, all the strange noises and occurrences stopped.

BABA MEETS AMANULLAH

Two days after Baba released the ghosts, Keki accompanied Baba and Mandali on a mast tour in Delhi. Baidul, at Baba's orders, had already prepared a list of the masts in the area. Baba first went to Fatahpuri bazaar where He contacted a mast. Next on the list was a mast living in the Ballimaran area whom Baba contacted. Baba then walked past the famous Sikh Gurudwara known as Shishganj. Although He did not go inside, He bowed and folded His hands from outside.

Baba then walked through the whole of Chandini Chowk and then along with all those accompanying Him, He entered the Gauri Shankar temple, which is dedicated to Lord Shiva. This temple is located opposite the Red Fort. Baba bowed down to Lord Shiva's idol and then they all came out. Baba explained that, being the Highest of the High, there was no need for Him to bow down at any of the holy places. But, he said, as time goes by such holy places lose their spiritual charge and that by bowing down at these places, He was recharging them spiritually. He also takes on all the sanskaras which have been deposited at such places by the thousands of devotees who visit them daily.

When Baba came out of the temple, He noticed a mast sleeping outside on the footpath. Vishnu asked Baba if he should wake up the mast, but Baba refused and asked him not to disturb the mast. Baidul then took all of them behind the Jama Masjid. Located at the crossing of the Jama Masjid and Chaori Bazaaar was a fifth plane mast whom Baba wanted to contact. His name was Amanullah. The mast was originally from Afghanistan and spoke Persian and Urdu.

Baba wanted to work with the mast in seclusion without any disturbance. As there was no place nearby, they took the mast along with them and went looking for a suitable place, which they finally found at the end of the Red Fort. This was the tomb of a great Muslim saint and was completely screened from outside by bamboo matting.

Baba took the mast inside the tomb and the rest of the Mandali stood guard outside. After finishing His work, Baba came out with the mast. He looked very happy and satisfied. Baba wanted to leave the mast back where they had found him. As they were walking back, the mast asked Baba where He would be going from Delhi. When Baba told him that He was going to Ajmer Sharif by the morning train, the mast insisted on accompanying Him.

Baba gave the mast ten rupees and asked him to buy his own ticket and come later. The mast took the money but insisted that he wanted to accompany Baba to Ajmer. Baba gave him another ten rupees and asked him to come separately.

By this time they had reached the spot where they had first found the mast. After a few minutes, Baba had Baidul request the mast to allow them to leave, but the mast refused to do so. After waiting for some time, Baba asked again but the mast wouldn't let them leave. Finally, Baba told the mast, "For God's sake, allow us to go."

Baidul was translating Baba's board and when he said, "For God's sake, allow us to go," the mast pointed towards Baba with his right hand and said that God was standing before him. The mast had recognized Baba's divinity. Whenever a mast recognized Baba's divinity, Baba would immediately leave.

Soon after this, they returned to Keki's house. Baba left Delhi the same day for Ajmer by the Ahmedabad Express which left at 9:25 am.

PURCHASE OF THE MAJRI MAFI PROPERTY

Keki wrote the following account about the purchase of the Majri Mafi property.

Baba's New Life started on 16th October, 1949. Before starting the New Life, Baba sat in seclusion in the Blue Bus at Meherazad for 40 days. This was known as the Great Seclusion and lasted from the 22nd of June 1949 to the 31st of July 1949. Baba had ordered all of His devotees to observe complete silence and partial fast from the 1st to the 31st of July. I went with my wife, Dhun, to Muzaffarnagar and stayed in the dak bungalow where we observed silence for it would have been difficult to do it in Delhi.

On 7th September 1949, I received a telegram from Baba which read as follows: "Come here immediately for one day. Baba." At that time, I was in Bombay and, on receiving the telegram, I informed Baba that I would reach Meherabad the next day. I traveled by train to Ahmednagar and reached there at 10 p.m. As it was late in the night, I did not want to disturb the Mandali and so I slept in the station waiting room. I did not know that Baba had instructed the Mandali to wait for my arrival at Meherabad and had also arranged for my stay there.

Early the next morning, Adi Sr came to the station looking for me. On seeing me, he asked me to accompany him to Meherabad immediately as Baba too would be arriving there at 8 a.m. Baba came sharply at 8 o'clock and held a meeting. He asked me about my health, my wife, Dhun, when I had come, where I had slept, etc., etc.

I told Him that I had slept at the station as it was late and I did not want to disturb the Mandali. On hearing this, Baba turned towards me and said, "Do you know there is a statue of a Parsi in Bombay known as ubbho Parsi (which means standing Parsi in English). Then He pointed towards Kaka Baria and said, "He is Nagar no Gando Parsi (meaning mad parsi). Lastly Baba pointed to me and said, "You are Delhi no chutiya parsi (meaning foolish parsi)." Baba had linked me on many occasions with the affairs of Delhi, making me feel that He was using me to do some inner work on Delhi.

Baba than informed me that He was leaving His old life and starting on the New Life Phase for which He planned to come and settle in North India. He asked me to find a suitable place near Roorkee, Haridwar, Rishikesh or Dehradun where He could stay. Baba explained that He wanted to live outside the town in a village which should be about five to six miles from the main town. He instructed me that no one should know about this plan, not even my wife.

I asked Baba if it would be all right to select a place near Dehradun for I knew people living there. Baba agreed. I asked Baba if I could take Keki

Nalawala's help. Baba agreed but warned me to see that no one besides him should know about it, not even his family.

I returned to Delhi immediately and the next day went to Dehradun where I met Keki and asked him for help. Unfortunately, he was unable to, and asked me to contact one of my dealer friends whose name was Balakram. On contacting Balakram, he agreed to help. He took me and Keki Nalawala to meet his friend who was living in a village called Majri Mafi which was about six miles from Dehradun, on the Haridwar road.

We were introduced to his friend, Shatrugan Kumar, who showed us three places. One was in the interior of a jungle which I rejected. The second place which he showed us was a small village school building near a pond. The third was his own house. I refused his last offer because he had no other place to go and would become homeless. So I asked him to show me yet another place. I liked what he showed me next because on this land there was a cottage with two small rooms and a verandah.

I took some photographs of this place and sent them to Baba, together with a detailed letter providing Him with the information about the places. On receiving my letter, Baba sent me a telegram which read as follows: "Contents of your telegram and descriptive letter made me happy. I prefer selection and purchase of site to be settled solely by you. Therefore, your presence at Ahmednagar absolutely necessary for one day. Come when convenient before 1st Oct to take money and instructions. Wire arrival. - Baba."

On receipt of this telegram, I went to Meherabad and met Baba who asked me to narrate everything in detail. I informed Him that there was no kitchen, bathroom, toilet or water facility and also there was no well nearby the cottage. Baba then asked me which place I preferred out of all the places Kumar had showed me. I told Baba that I liked the small cottage.

At this, Baba said that He too liked that place and asked me to settle everything for the purchase of this property for which He gave me Rs 28,000. I returned to Delhi and the very next day left for Dehradun. I met Kumar and told him that Baba wanted to purchase the land with the cottage. Finally the sale deed of the land with the cottage was executed in the joint names of 1) Ardeshir S. Baria (Kaka Baria) 2) Eruch B. Jessawala and 3) Keki A. Desai. Our professions were mentioned as agriculturists.

The sale of the land with cottage cost Rs 8,500. However, there was a standing crop of sugarcane and wheat for which the owner was paid Rs 500 extra. In addition to this, a well was dug, a soak pit toilet was built, a hut was built for the men Mandali and also repair works were carried out. The total cost came to Rs 16,385.

After all the work was completed, I informed Baba and He sent a telegram in reply on 7th Oct. which read as follows: "Be at Pimpalgaon on 9th. Baba." As directed, I went to Ahmednagar and Adi Sr came to receive me at the station. He drove me in his car to Meherazad (Pimpalgaon) where I met Baba. As Kaka Baria had gone to Bombay, Baba asked me to sleep in his room.

After finishing the evening meal, Baba asked me to accompany Him to see His bedroom which was located upstairs at that time. I went with Baba and Baidul, who carried a hurricane Lantern, as there was no electricity then. Baba Himself showed me His room which was a very simple one.

Next day Adi took us in his car to Meherabad and, on the way, we had a discussion with Baba about the property. As Baba was disposing off everything that He and the Mandali possessed in the old life before starting His New Life, I requested Baba to give me something belonging to Him as a souvenir.

Baba had given specific instructions saying that "Nothing should be on My name except the Tomb on Meherabad Hill." In response to my request, Baba gave me a mattress. He would sit on this mattress while doing His mast work in Meherabad. After lunch, I left for Delhi.

BABA TAKES BHIKSHA IN BENARAS

After starting His New Life, Baba and the New Life companions came from Belgaum to Benares on 15th November 1949. They stayed at a place called Nati Imli. On 29th November, He sent Keki Desai the following telegram, "Be at Benares cantonment station on 8th Dec definitely to leave Benaras on 10th with our luggage to Haridwar property. Acknowledge this telegraphically to William Donkin care of Station Master Benaras Cantonment. Eruch Jessawala."

Baba used to refer to the Majri Mafi property as the Haridwar property. What follows is described in Keki's own words.

"As per Baba's instructions, I reached Benaras and met Dr. Donkin and Padri at the Cantonment Station. Padri had come from Ahmednagar with a caravan as per Baba's orders. Baba had instructed Don to narrate all the incidents of the New Life from 16th Oct. upto the date of His arrival in Benaras to Padri. Baba then asked Padri to share all this information with me when I reached Benaras and I was supposed to share it with Harjiwan Lal, Kain, Kishan Singh and Todi Singh in Delhi."

In the New Life, Baba carried a very small amount of money. In order to raise extra money for expenses, Baba sent His and His companions' extra clothes in a trunk to a Baba lover, Dr. S. Nath, and asked him to give Rs 1,000 for it. Dr. Nath was a leading eye surgeon of Uttar Pradesh and Dr. Khare, his friend, was working in Benaras Hindu Univeristy. During Baba's New Life phase, Baba often sent the companions to both these Baba lovers, instructing them to provide for their various needs. They did this willingly, although they did not know of Baba's identity in the beginning.

They served Baba in every respect, fulfilling all His wishes. In order to reward them, Baba decided to take bhiksha from both these families. He took bhiksha from Dr. Nath's family on 24th Nov 1949 and, on the next day, from Dr. Khare's family. Thus Baba gave His darshan to both these families. It was at the time of taking Baba's darshan that they recognized Baba, for Baba had kept His identity a secret all along.

Baba then asked Keki to carry His and the companions luggage from Benaras to Dehradun by train and then to Majri Mafi. Baba asked Keki to pay Rs 500 for the extra luggage and also for His train tickets. In exchange for this, Baba asked all the companions to take off their watches, which He then handed over to Keki asking him to sell them and recover the Rs 500 which he had paid. Only Adi Sr, Dr. Donkin and Mani were asked to keep their watches.

Keki kept Dr. Goher's watch and disposed of the rest as desired by Baba. The luggage consisted of thirteen packages, out of which three steel trunks contained Baba's personal belongings. Baba instructed Keki to be very careful of them. Keki took the luggage by train to Dehradun and from there to the Haridwar property (Majri Mafi).

Kaikobad Dastur, who was living at Keki Desai's place in Delhi at the beginning of the New Life, as per Baba's order, had now shifted to Majri Mafi. Baba also instructed Kaikobad to keep an eye on His and the companions' luggage. As he was living alone at Majri Mafi, his meals were served by Shatrugan Kumar, for which Baba gave Kumar Rs 100 per month.

BABA'S STAY IN MORADABAD

Baba sent Adi Sr. from Jaunpur (U.P.) to Keki Desai's place in Delhi on 18th Dec 1949. He instructed him to take Keki and Harjiwan Lal's help to find a suitable place in Moradabad for Himself and His companions. As per Baba's instructions, Keki met Harjiwan Lal and asked him to be present at his place the next day at 4 a.m. to accompany them for the task that Baba had given them.

Harjiwan Lal did not show up the next day and after waiting till 4:30 a.m., Adi Sr. and Keki left for Moradabad. They got there at 10 a.m. and first went to the Grand hotel where they checked in. After depositing their luggage, they went searching for a suitable place for Baba. In spite of looking for it the whole day, they were unsuccessfully.

The next day, Harjiwan Lal came and, coincidentally, he too checked in at the Grand Hotel. As Keki and Adi had left the hotel in the early moring they did not run into each other. Harjiwan Lal decided to go to a local barber for a shave and inquired with him if he knew of any place in the city where a big party of pilgrims with some animals could stay without any disturbance.

The barber mentioned a place known as Ramlila Grounds and also gave the owner's name and address to Harjiwan Lal who went and met the owner. He asked the owner to allow a group of pilgrims on their way to Haridwar, along with a few animals to stay on his property. (When Baba left Benaras on 12th Dec. 1949 to begin the walk to Dehradun He had some animals which He had acquired during His stay in Benaras. Baba had a white horse, two donkeys, a camel, a cow with a calf, two bullocks and an English bull.) The owner readily agreed to it.

Adi and Keki returned unsuccessfully to the hotel where they met Harjiwan Lal who gave them the good news. Baba had specifically asked Adi Sr. to take Harjiwan Lal's help for this work. In spite of leaving Harjiwan Lal behind, in the end it was he who accomplished the task. All three of them went to inspect the place the next day and approved it. Adi Sr. however asked Harjiwan Lal to make some enclosures.

While in Moradabad, Adi got a telegram from Baba from Jaunpur informing him that He and the companions would reach Moradabad on the 22nd of December by the Doon Express. Harjiwan Lal returned to Delhi whereas Keki had to stay in Moradabad with Adi.

As no one was supposed to see Baba in the New Life, Adi went alone to receive Baba at the station and he brought Baba and the companions to the Ramlila Grounds. Baba sent a message through

Adi to Keki asking Keki to see Him between 1-2 p.m. that same day.

When Keki arrived, he saw Aloba fetching water but turned his face and looked the other way as it was Baba's order not to interact or look at any of the Mandali. When Keki met Baba, He explained through Eruch that if by the 15th of January the Haridwar Property (Majri Mafi) was not ready, then Keki should hire a bungalow in Dehradun, or nearby, from the 15th January till the end of February. The rent for this period of one and a half months should be between Rs 200 and Rs 500.

At this point, when Baba gave these instructions, repair work was going on at Majri Mafi. After giving these instructions, Baba showed Keki the room from outside where the women Mandali were staying. Just near the steps leading to the women's room was a small tent in which Baba was staying. Baba instructed Keki to inquire from Delhi's Kabari bazaar (flea market) if such tents were available for He wanted twelve of them. Baba mentioned that the tent in which He was living was given by Dr. Donkin who had got it during his service in the Second World War. ·

After returning to Delhi, Keki tried looking for the tent but could not find any. One tent merchant, however, agreed to make similar tents. Keki informed Baba about this and Baba replied through

Adi telling Keki to get one water proof tent prepared and get it to Dehradun on 12th January for His approval.

Baba stayed in Moradabad from the 22nd December till the 31st. This period was called the vacuum period by Baba. During this period, there was to be no begging, no langoti life, no labor phase and no wearing of the kafni. 25th December was Mehera's birthday. As Keki Desai was not present, he requested Adi to give a birthday cake to Baba as bhiksha from him.

Keki was in Delhi when he received a letter dated 26th December from Baba in which He mentioned that He and His companions would be leaving Moradbad on foot for Dehradun on the first of January and would reach there on the 12th . Baba asked Keki to arrange for bungalows by the 12th. Also Padri would give Keki Rs 10,000 which he should take to Dehradun on the 12th.

After making payments for the new shed, the construction of the toilets, bathroom doors and also for the bungalow rents, the remaining amount he had to give to Baba for the animals. Baba insisted that the Majri Mafi property should be ready, definitely, by the end of February 1950.

Baba and the companions left Moradabad on foot for Dehradun as planned on the first. They halted at various small places after walking a distance of 10-14 miles each day. While halting at a small town in Nahtaur in Bijnor District (U.P.), Baba sent a telegram on January 7th to Keki as a reminder which read: "We arrive Dehradun station on 12th Jan. If bungalows not settled arrange suitable camping grounds till bungalows are secured. Arrange through Nalawala and others food for 20 persons for 7 days purely in bhiksha. Also arrange through bhiksha conveyance for transport of luggage and ladies from station to our bungalow or camping place--Eruch Jessawala."

As was Baba's habit to send repeated reminders, He sent another telegram on the 10th through Eruch from Najibabad in Bijnor District as follows: "Definitely arriving 10th morning by Howrah Express. Wire immediately care of Station Master Najibabad what accommodation arranged. Eruch"

Since the Haridwar property was not ready, Keki asked Harjiwan Lal to arrange for a bungalow to rent for Baba and His companions where they could stay for a few days before shifting to Majri Mafi. Harjiwan Lal managed to rent a bungalow which was called Mrs. Pratt's bungalow, located at No 4 New Cantonment Rd in Dehradun.

TODI SINGH GIVES BHIKSHA

Todi Singh, who lived in Aligarh, came to know about Baba's New Life activities through Kishan Singh. Todi Singh and his son, Gajraj Singh, met Keki when he was living in Keki Nalawala's house in Dehradun on the 11th of January, or one day before Baba's arrival. He came with two cans of pure ghee which he wanted to give to Baba in bhiksha and asked Keki to deliver them.

Keki Nalawala, Burjor Chacha and Eruch Mistry, along with Todi Singh and his son, went to the station the next day with Keki Desai to welcome and receive Baba. As it was Baba's strict order that no one should see Him in the New Life, Keki asked all of them to wait outside the railway station

Baba and His companions arrived by the Doon Express at about 10 a.m. Keki received them and they all went to the waiting room. In a shortwhile Shatrugan Kumar, along with his servant, as per Baba's orders, arrived with food for Baba and the companions on his motorcycle. Keki told Baba about Todi Singh's bhiksha and also about all the ones who were waiting outside hoping that Baba would agree to give them darshan

Baba agreed to do so and the food was served by Baba Himself to everyone present. After eating, Baba and the companions left for Mrs Pratt's bungalow.

Baba instructed Kumar to provide meals for Him and His companions during their temporary stay in Dehradun and told him it should be cooked using the pure ghee given by Todi Singh. Baba told Kumar to deliver the lunch himself but said that Keki Desai would pick up the dinner each day at Kumar's house

Half of Mrs Pratt's bungalow was occupied by Baba and the ladies. The men companions occupied the out houses. The other half of the bungalow was occupied by an old English couple, Mr and Mrs Angelo. The couple became interested in Baba and asked Keki to arrange for them to meet Baba. Keki informed Baba of their wish and He readily agreed

On the appointed day, Baba put on a white kafni and asked Keki how he looked. Keki replied that he look like Christ in the white kafni along with His long flowing hair. Baba did this for the benefit of the couple as they were Christians

Baba shifted from Mrs Pratt's bungalow to Majri Mafi on the 15th of January in the evening. They were accommodated in a big house known as Mahantji Ki Haveli which was about a mile from the Majri Mafi property. The Majri Mafi property was not yet ready and hence Shatrugan Kumar requested his friend who was the village Mahant(headman), name Jamnadas, who owned this haveli, to give it for Baba's use. Mahant agreed and also helped Kumar's family in preparing food for Baba and the companions. Baba stayed in this haveli from the 15th of January to the 2nd of March

An interestng incident took place between Baba and Mahant which is as follows

Jamnadas, the Mahant (head man) of the village of Manjri Mafi had been arrested for shooting and killing 2 villagers in a dispute. He was temporarily released as he was sick with tuberculosis and he was supposed to report back to prison on June 17, 1950 to continue serving his sentence.

On April 20, 1950, Baba asked him, "Would you sincerely and faithfully carry out 2 instructions that I give you?" Jamnadas said that he would.

Baba said , "Then, don't worry in the least about your permanent release untill the very last minute of your going back to prison on June 17th.And, every night before going to bed offer this hearfelt prayer, "O God, I leave my fate in Your Hands!"

Jamnadas agreed to follow those instructions. Then Baba said, "I feel inwardly that if you obey these instructions faithfully, God will not fail you!"

On June 14th, a government order was received that Jamnadas was officially released from prison.

Baba was the one to give him the news, and he attributed it all to Baba's Nazar.

BABA SCOLDS KEKI

Baba had given Keki Desai the duty of bringing dinner for Himself and His companions from Shatrugan Kumar's house each day. One day, Baba instructed Keki to bring whatever dinner was ready and to return immediately. He asked Keki not to wait at Kumar's place for anything.

On reaching Kumar's house, Keki informed them about Baba's order. They, however, told Keki that it was their plan to make puris and, as they had to make 100 puris, it would take time. They asked him to wait and Keki, reluctantly, agreed because they were already in the process of preparing the puris.

After collecting the dinner, on the way to Majri Mafi, each day Keki would buy bread from a local bakery for Baba. On this particular day, Keki, who was already late, got delayed further because the tongawalla got lost.

Baba was getting anxious and would repeatedly ask everyone as to why Keki had not arrived yet. When Keki finally got there, Baba asked him why there had been a delay and Keki explained the whole situation.

The food basket was sent over to the ladies' side as usual. The ladies took out their share and sent the rest for the men companions. As Baba could not take solid food, only soft rice and dal would be prepared and sent for Him in the same basket. It so happened that because of the delay in preparing the puris, Kumar and his wife and servant had packed everything in a hurry and, in the process, had forgotten Baba's food.

Keki was having his meal with the men Mandali when Baba came and started scolding Keki. Baba was upset with Keki for having broken His order by waiting at Kumar's place and also forgetting to check whether Kumar had given His food or not. Baba told Keki, "You are nicely eating your meal whereas I will have to remain hungry."

Keki was very upset and could not eat after that. Seeing this, Dr Nilu said to Keki, after Baba had left, to not worry and to continue eating for it was Baba's habit to scold everyone.

Baba returned after some time and told Keki that the next day he should go straight from Nalawala's place to Kumar's house without seeing Him first, as was his daily practice. Baba told Keki to tell Kumar and his family that the puri preparation was an unnecessary hardship for the women and also that they had forgotten to send Baba's food.

During Baba's stay in Dehradun, Keki would stay at Keki Nalawala's house. However, he would spend the whole day with Baba and the Mandali and also have his meals with them. So when Keki returned back to Nalawala's house, Baba sent Vishnu at 10 p.m. with a message for Keki that he should see Baba first next morning before going to Kumar's place. Baba also told Keki to sleep well.

The next morning, Keki met Baba as instructed and spent the day with Him. Baba was no longer upset with him and Keki remembered how Baba had scolded him on an earlier occasion in Agra and explained to him later that by doing so He was cutting off the bad sanskaras of His close ones. Keki felt that Baba had done the same thing this time.

When Keki reached Kumar's place and conveyed Baba's message, everyone was surprised for no one had realized until then that Baba's food had not been sent.

BABA'S BIRTHDAY CELEBRATIONS

Baba had by now shifted along with the companions to the Majri Mafi property as it was ready. According to the Parsi calendar, Baba's birthday in 1950 was celebrated on the 12th of February. Baba asked Keki Nalawala to write a letter to Keki Desai asking him to come to Majri Mafi on the morning of the 12th to take part in His birthday celebrations, and to stay there for five days. Baba, however, made it clear that Keki should only come if he did not have any important work in his office or home.

Since Keki was tied up with office work, he informed Baba that he would come after completing it. Keki reached Majri Mafi on the 23rd. On the 25th, Baba's birthday was celebrated according to the English calendar. Baba served food to everyone with His own hands. All would get up daily between 3 am and 4 am to get ready to assemble in the store room (where tea would be served) exactly at 5 am. Before taking tea, Dr Nilu would recite a couplet in Sanskrit in praise of all the past Avatars in which Baba took part by standing with all the companions. Baba's face would be calm, serene and full of luster during the recital.

On the 28th, Dr Donkin's consulting clinic was inaugurated in Dehradun for which Baba asked all to assemble. Baba had decided to start a new phase of the New Life called the Labor Phase, in which the men Mandali were expected to do hard labor and support themselves from the money earned. Dr. Donkin decided that as a doctor he could run a clinic and earn money that way. Ironically, no one would go to Dr. Donkin's clinic whereas there was a clinic nearby run by an Indian which was full of patients. In desperation, Donkin would sometimes plead with the Nalawalas to get him some patients.

On the 1st of March, Baba took a bath with water drawn from the Ganges which was brought by Baidul. Before taking the bath, at about 1 p.m., Baba cut a lock of hair from each companion's head with a pair of scissors. At 4 p.m., Keki Nalawala gave cooked food to Baba in bhiksha.

On the 3rd of March, Baba asked the men companions to wash their own feet. Baba then placed is head on their feet. Baba then asked their pardon for having hurt their feelings, and also forgave them for any mistake committed by them. Addressing the companions, Baba said, "During the period between 16th October 1949 and 1st March 1950, I have committed consciously and deliberately one big mistake and I want the companions to kick me so that God forgives me." Baba never disclosed what this big mistake was. Thereupon He made the companions kick him.

During Keki Desai's stay with Baba in Dehradun,

Baba distributed items offered by Mr. Kain in bhiksha to all His companions. It consisted of ready made striped cotton shirts, banians, small cakes of Lux toilet soap and small combs. Keki also received his share from Baba. As no one was allowed to meet Baba in the New Life, Baba had asked Keki to bring Kain's bhiksha with him when he arrived in Dehradun.

BABA GOES TO MOTICHUR

On March 3rd , Baba, along with Gustadji, Eruch, Baidul, Aloba,Keki and Nalawala left Majri Mafi to go to Harrawala railway station, which was about 2 ½ miles away. They left at 12:30 pm on foot while the luggage was transported in a bullock cart. While walking, Baba asked Keki to hold an umbrella over His head. When they got to the station, they went to the waiting room where Baba sat on a chair and the rest of them sat on a bench.

As there was still time for the train to come from Dehardun, Baba asked Eruch and Keki to bring tea for all from a small village teashop nearby. A wooden plank was hanging from the roof of the waiting room. Baba pointed to it and said it looked like the sword of Damocles. Baba then put His index finger on His forehead and said to Keki, "You are very lucky to have your one foot in the Old Life and the other in the New Life with Me.'

The train tickets were purchased as per Baba's order on the Amritsar Passenger train by Mr. Nalawala. Two berths were reserved for Baba and party in the third class from Dehradun. Harrawala, being a small station on the Haridwar — Dehradun section, had no proper platform. When the train arrived, Baba and party got on board. However, as the halt was only for two minutes, Baidul was left behind, along with half the luggage.

When the train departed, two beggars came to Baba's compartment. One of them was an old blind man led by a small boy. The blind man was singing a Hindi song, "Ram chale banwas Ayodhya roye," which means "when Ram left for exile, Ayodhya wept." On hearing the words, Keki pointed to Baba for Baba too had exiled Himself from the world and was now leading a wandering life, just like Lord Rama. Baba gestured to Keki to keep quiet and also asked him to give the beggars some coins.

On reaching Raiwala junction station, Baba and party got down. The rest of the journey to Motichur was done by truck. Baba sat next to the driver and the rest of the companions were standing behind in the truck along with the luggage.. They reached Motichur cottage at 4:50 p.m.

Motichur cottage had only one small room which was occupied by Baba and all the others slept outside in the open verandah. Baba's room had no furniture, not even a cot, so Baba slept on the floor. Baba made this place His temporary headquarters for His Kumbh Mela work. Baba swept His own room without taking any help from anyone and arranged all things Himself.

In the evening, Baba served all with His own hands chapattis and cooked potatoes which the ladies at Marji Mafi had prepared and given to Baba for the journey. After serving the food, Baba wanted to wash

His hands. He looked at Keki and Keki immediately tore the wrapper of the lux soap which Baba had earlier given to him as his share from Kain's bhiksha. Baba washed His hands with the soap and returned it to Keki who preserved it as a souvenir. Later tea was served to all.

On the 4th , Baba took a bath, after which He sat in seclusion in a grass hut specially made for Him. Baba asked Nalawala and Keki to sit on watch duty outside the hut. After thirty minutes, Baba came out, having finished His seclusion work. Baba informed everyone that they would be getting one meal a day consisting of dal and chapattis. Morning tea with little milk would be served. Breakfast would consist of left over chapattis from the previous evening, if any were left, and afternoon tea would be served without milk.

Baba then swept His room and rearranged the things. Baba also washed His own clothes and cleaned His own utensils. Baidul, who was left behind, arrived that day in a truck with the remaining luggage from the Harrawala Station. After their meal, Baba asked Keki to leave for Delhi and Nalawala for Dehradun.

BABA CONTACTS SADHUS AND MAHATMAS

Baba wrote a letter through Eruch to Keki in Delhi from Motichur dated 28/3/1950 in which He asked Keki to be present in Motichur on the 31st if possible and convenient. Baba further said that Keki should ensure that his work did not suffer in the least by his coming. Keki left Delhi by the night train on the 30th reaching Haridwar early the next morning. Keki took a cycle rickshaw and headed towards Motichur cottage.

On the way, he saw Baba with Eruch, Pendu, Gustadji and Baidul going on foot to contact sadhus, saints and mahatmas who had come to take part in the Kumbh Mela from all over India. Keki was carrying a huge rice bag which he brought from Delhi for Baba. Baba asked Keki what it was and Keki explained that he had brought a rice bag as there was a scarcity of it in the country due to which the same was not available in Dehradun. Baba was pleased and asked Keki to put his luggage in the Motichur cottage and return to join them.

Daily, Baba, along with the men Mandali and Keki would leave Motichur at the break of dawn and go on foot to Haridwar and surrounding places to contact sadhus. Pendu kept record of the daily contacts. After finishing the work that took six to seven hours, they would return to the cottage by bus. If a bus was not available, then they would walk.

Sometimes, Baba would be so tired that He would actually be dragging His feet.

On reaching the cottage, Baba would rest for some time. Later, they all would play different games like marbles, gilli danda and cards. While playing cards (la risqué) Keki felt happy because Baba always chose to keep him as a partner for His group.

In Motichur, Baba asked Keki to send a telegram to Todi Singh in Aligarh which said, "Come to my Delhi house on 4th April for 1 day." Baba instructed Keki after that to leave Motichur for Delhi on the 3rd with points which He gave him to discuss with Harjiwan Lal, Kain, Kishan Singh and Todi Singh.

Baba told Keki that after finishing His work, he should return to Majri Mafi on the 10th. Baba finished His work at Haridwar on the 4th and left Motichur for good the next day for Majri Mafi. Baba contacted a total of 10,000 sadhus during the Kumbh Mela.

Keki returned to Majri Mafi on the 10th, after completing Baba's work. On the 11th, Baba called a meeting of the companions which was very important. In this meeting, Baba decided that from the 1st of May, all the companions would come under the new plan in which they would have to earn their livelihood. It was decided to hold another meeting on the 15th to decide on the future course of action.

BABA GOES TO SEE THE KUMBH MELA

On the 12th , Baba, along with Eruch and the ladies, left Majri Mafi for Dehradun railway station by the station wagon. From there they all went to Haridwar by rail to see the Kumbh Mela.

The 13th of April was considered the most auspicious day, when thousands of sadhus and pilgrims were to come from all over India to take a dip in the holy Ganges. Keki and the rest of the men companions, who were left behind, started their journey that day in the early morning. They walked on foot towards the Dehradun railway station which was about 5 miles away.

On reaching the station, they met Burjor Chacha, Keki Nalawala, Dr. Donkin and Eruch Mistry (also called Elcha). Due to the pilgrim season, the train was over crowded. However, they managed to board it and reached Haridwar Station at 11 am. From the station they went to Mr. Sansarchand Goel's Mansion, where Baba and the ladies were staying. Mrs Nalawala, Mrs Shatrugan Kumar and Mrs Chacha were also staying with the ladies.

Baba called all the companions and asked Don to read out His message which was as follows: "May God forgive us all companions in the New Life for any mistake committed consciously or unconsciously towards Him or towards each other. I forgive you companions wholeheartedly for any mistake done to Me and ask forgiveness of you companions if I have in any way hurt your feelings. On behalf of Myself and you companions of the New Life, I ask God to forgive us if conditions of New Live have been consciously or unconsciously broken. For Myself I ask God to give Me the strength to stick to my oath till the very end and fulfill all conditions of the New Life 100% with His help."

When Don finished reading, Baba touched the feet of every companion. Baba's face was calm and serene throughout. Afterwards, Baba took everyone on the terrace from where they could have a beautiful panoramic view of the Ganges. Baba then told the men companions that they could go and see the Kumbh Mela processions and visit places connected with it if they so wished. He warned them to stay together so that they were not lost or separated from each in the sea of humanity.

The men Mandali did as Baba asked and returned in the evening. Baba had planned to leave Haridwar with all His companions the next day. However, He changed His mind suddenly and decided to return to Majri Mafi in the middle of the night. While undertaking the journey, a humorous incident happened.

Baba had instructed all to stay together. When the train arrived, Dr. Nilu saw an empty compartment and got in. He was tired, so he fell asleep. All the men Mandali, along with Baba, boarded a different compartment. When Baba and the companions got down at Harrawala Station, Dr. Nilu was still sleeping and did not get down until the train reached Dehradun.

Nilu woke up and got down but had to walk all the way to Majri Mafi, a distance of five miles in the pitch dark of night, through the jungle. He got to Majri Mafi at two in the morning.

The next morning, he told everyone what had happened and said that while passing through the jungle he was not frightened of the wild beasts but of the ghosts. All had a good laugh.

On the 15th , Baba held a meeting. At the end of the meeting, Baba instructed Eruch and Keki to leave in the morning for Delhi by bus. Baba wanted them to find suitable accommodations for the companions in Delhi as they were going to start a new plan of hard labor.

Keki and Eruch left Majri Mafi at 8 a.m. and, on completion of the work, Eruch returned immediately. Keki returned on the 28th . Once there, he gave Baba a complete report of the work carried out in Delhi. Baba then held a meeting of the companions and told them that the stay in Majri Mafi was impractical so He was planning to shift to Delhi. He decided to sell

of the Majri Mafi property and asked Shatrugan
Kumar to find a suitable buyer.

SALE OF MAJRI MAFI PROPERTY

Baba wanted to sell the Majri Mafi property for which He asked Kain, Kishan Singh, Todi Singh and Harjiwan Lal to be present in Majri Mafi on the 13th. Baba told them His wish and said that either they should buy it collectively or individually. He said that He wanted Rs 7000 for the property, although a much larger amount had been spent on it.

On hearing this, Keki was happy as he was hoping that one of the Baba lovers from Delhi would purchase the property and preserve it for posterity so that lovers from all over the world could come for darshan to one of the most sacred spots connected with Baba.

But all four of the group began looking at each other and appeared unsure about purchasing the property. Finally they expressed their inability to buy it. On hearing this, Baba became very angry. He pointed to Harjiwan Lal and said, "You were ready to cut your throat for My work. Now what happened?"

Turning to Todi Singh, He said, "You said that for My work you would even become naked. Have you forgotten those words of yours"

Baba, who was still angry, asked them to go away and they left dejectedly. Seeing them refuse to buy the property, Keki was upset and pleaded with Baba to give them one more chance to buy it. Baba asked Keki to call them back. Keki was so excited on hearing this that he ran barefoot on the road to call them back.

They had already reached the main road by the time Keki caught up with them and informed them of Baba's order. Baba told them not to worry about the property as He had already decided that this property should go to an outsider . Baba embraced them and then sent them away. They went away happily.

The Majri Mafi property was purchased by a photographer from Dehradun, Mr Goel.

Baba had set May 1st as the date for a special bhiksha. All the men companions put on white kafni and green turbans and assembled in the cottage. Baba came to the cottage at 6:30 am in a white kafni. He asked Kaka Baria and Nilu to help Him put on the green turban. Baba's face was full of luster and His eyes were shining.

At 6:45 a.m. Baba and the companions of the new plan went out to beg. They walked a distance of two miles and came to the dry sandy river called Rispana. Mr and Mrs Nalawala, Mr and Mrs Burjor Chacha and Shatrugan Kumar and his mother were supposed to arrive from Dehradun with the bhiksha. Baba asked Keki to find out whether they had arrived.

On checking, Keki found that they had already gotten there and were waiting under the shade of a neem tree for Baba. Keki told this to Baba and He sent Keki back to them to tell them to bring the bhiksha. The bhiksha consisted of containers of food which they offered to Baba one at a time. Baba accepted it all and the containers were then carried by the companions on their heads all the way to the cottage with Baba leading the way.

On arriving at the cottage, Baba told them that this was to be the last bhiksha. Baba served everyone the food with His own hands. Mr Goel, who had purchased Majri Mafi, was also present and had the good fortune to be served by Baba. All activities at Majri Mafi came to a close from that day.

Eruch, Nilu, Murli, Aloba, Kaka Baria, Gustadji, Pendu, Baidul, Vishnu, Dr. Donkin and Sadashiv Patil joined the New Plan Group by Baba's order. Baba, along with the four women companions, Baidul and Vishnu shifted from Majri Mafi to No 29 Lytton Rd in Dehradun on the 10th . Baidul and Vishnu were both to serve Baba and the women for which Baba paid them Rs 50 each as their salary per month. Food was also cooked and supplied to them by the women. They both lived at Burjor Chacha's place in Dehradun.

GHEE BUSINESS IN DELHI

Baba invited suggestions from the companions about what business they should do which would be 100% honest. Baidul suggested opening a laundry, whereas Eruch felt that opening a hair cutting salon would be good. Baba rejected these suggestions and said, "Let's call Todi Singh. He will find a solution to the problem." Todi Singh was called and when Baba asked his opinion, he suggested that a ghee business should be started. Baba liked this idea.

The companions consisting of Gustadji, Eruch, Kaka Baria, Kaikobad, Pendu, Aloba, Nilu, Murli and Don, left Majri Mafi for Delhi on the 10th of May by the night train from the Dehradun railway station and arrived the next morning in Delhi to start the hard labor phase.

As no proper accommodation was available for the companions to do the ghee business in Delhi, by Baba's orders, they were all accommodated at Keki Desai's place on Nicholson Rd, Kashmiri Gate. Keki was all alone in the house as his wife, Dhun, had gone to Navsari. Baba asked Dhun to extend her stay there so that the Mandali could stay in their house.

Baba also asked Dhun's cousin, Burjor Gai, who was living at Keki's place, to vacate it. As Keki's neighbors' flat was empty, and the keys were with Keki, Burjor was moved there. Baba allowed Burjor to meet the companions if he so wished.

Gustadji, Kaka Baria and Eruch slept in the main hall. Dr. Nilu and Dr. Donkin occupied the bed room which was usually used by Baba when He stayed there. The second bedroom was given to Kaikobad Dastur, whose main work was to take Baba's name one lakh times a day. Aloba, Murli and Pendu stayed on the front verandah and Keki slept on the back verandah. Todi Singh, who helped out with the ghee business according to Baba's wish, would visit periodically. During his visits, which would be for a few days, he would sleep on the back verandah as well. Baba chose Todi Singh because he had a factory where ghee was made.

Aloba was given the charge of the kitchen and had to cook for the companions. Dr. Nilu had to grind spices like garlic, ginger, chillies, etc to be added to the food. He had to grind it on a grinding stone slab with a small grinding stone. Kaikobad Dastur and Gustadji were exempted from doing any work due to their old age. Kaka Baria handled cash and Eruch kept the accounts. Apart from all these duties, everyone had to help out in the preparation of ghee, which consisted of churning the cream in a big wooden drum.

For the purpose of preparing ghee, Todi Singh brought two big cans of cream from a town called Haldwani in U.P. He also brought the necessary items such as a large wooden drum, big utensils and a large stove which was needed for preparing the ghee. He had to go to his factory at Aligarh to bring all these things.

The opening ceremony was done on the 12th of May by Kaka Baria who turned the handle on the wooden drum. Todi Singh taught the companions how to prepare ghee. First the cream was put in the wooden drum. The cream had to be churned with a wooden handle which the companions did by turns. When the cream turned into butter, the butter would be removed from the wooden drum and put into the utensil which would then be heated on a big stove.

As the butter was heated, it had to be stirred continuously. After stirring for a long time, ghee would finally be ready. All this had to be carried out in the open courtyard in the blistering summer heat during the month of May.

The companions were totally exasperated during the preparation. Every alternate day, Todi Singh would go to a different cream collecting center in Uttar Pradesh to bring more cream. When a sufficient quantity of ghee was made, it was poured into tin cans of different sizes which were purchased from a local tin factory.

Donkin prepared the logo and the business was named the " Nav Jiwan Ghee Company" which means New Life Ghee company. Labels were prepared and put on the tin cans. Also a sign board was prepared and put outside the house for people to see.

GHEE BUSINESS CLOSES DOWN

When the final product, in the form of ghee tins was ready, the companions tried to market it to Delhi wholesalers. However, no one showed any interest in the product even though it was the purest ghee because the price was high. The wholesalers in Delhi were marketing adulterated ghee which was sold at a far lower price and they felt that no one would buy this expensive product.

Baba was told what was happening and He replied that He would come to Delhi and settle the matter. He also asked Keki to come and meet Him on the 22nd which Keki did. On the 23rd , Baba, Baidul and Keki left Dehradun for Delhi by the morning bus and reached Delhi at 4 p.m. Kishan Singh and Harjiwan Lal came with their cars to take Baba to Mr. Kain's house. Generally Baba stayed at Keki's during His Delhi visits but, due to the ghee business and the companions living at Keki's place, the house was a complete mess and it would have been inconvenient for Baba to stay there. So it was decided He would stay at Kain's.

Eruch had also come to receive Baba and he left with Baba for Kain's place in Harjiwan Lal's car. Baidul went with Keki to Keki's house. Baba had informed Keki that He would come on the next day at 8 a.m. and ordered all four Delhi Baba lovers: Kain, Kishan Singh, Harjiwan Lal and Todi Singh, to be present at 8 a.m. as well. Baba arrived exactly at 8 a.m. and all the companions received Him

Before the meeting began, Baba asked Keki to go with Todi Singh to the local fruit market and bring a big watermelon. When the watermelon was brought, Baba took a knife and asked everyone to guess how many pieces would come out of the watermelon. Everyone gave a different number. However, it was Todi Singh whose guess of 27 turned out to be correct. When Baba cut the watermelon, exactly 27 pieces came out of it. Baba gave everyone one piece, except for Todi Singh who got an extra piece as a reward for guessing the correct number.

Baba sat cross-legged on the floor and everyone sat with Him in a semi circle. The meeting was conducted by Baba and Eruch gave a complete report to Baba of the whole situation. Baba tightened His left hand into a fist and slapped His right hand on top of it as if putting a seal to it.

Baba then ordered Mr. Kain to buy the entire stock of ghee for Rs 1000 which Kain did. The total value of the ghee stock was much higher than Rs 1000 but, as the companions would say, "When the Avatar does business, you always lose out."

Baba stayed the whole day at Keki's place and had his lunch which was prepared by Aloba. Baba removed some of His food and gave it to Keki to eat as His Prasad. Kishan Singh requested Baba to spend the night at his house to which Baba agreed, so Baba spent the night there.

The next day, the 25th , Baba came again to Keki's flat, had His lunch and later left with a few of the companions and Keki for Harjiwan Lal's house for tea. Later on, Baba instructed Keki to accompany Him and Kaka Baria to Dehradun. Kaka Baria was not keeping good health so Baba took him to Dehradun.

BABA CONTACTS MASTS

Baba left Delhi on the morning of the 26th in Harjiwan Lal's car for Dehradun. Dhun's cousin, Burjor Gai, had prepared food and packed it and given it to Baba to have on the journey. Baba was accompanied by Kaka Baria, Baidul and Keki.

They first halted at Ghaziabad where Baba served food to everyone. After lunch, Baba sent Baidul to find some masts. Only one mast was found and Baba made a contact with him near a mosque. The next halt was at Meerut. Baba asked Baidul to find the where abouts of Merwan, the spiritual chargeman of Meerut. Baidul inquired and learned that Merwan would be at Surajkund (where dead bodies were burnt) at a particular time.

So Baba and all of them went there at the specified time and looked for him, but he was no where to be found. On further inquiry, it was learned that Merwan would go every day at 2 p.m. to eat pakoras (a deep fried battered snack) at a certain shop in a place called Sohrab Gate.

They all went to the shop and even waited there for half an hour. However, on that day, Merwan decided not to appear. There, the locals, who knew Merwan, advised them to go to the District Court as he had been seen there by someone. When Baba and party reached the District Court, Merwan, who had been there, had just left.

Baba was eager to contact Merwan. The mast, however, kept avoiding Baba as he knew that Baba would put additional responsibility on his shoudlers which he did not want. Baba finally gave up the idea of contacting him and left Meerut for Muzaffanagar.

On the way, one of their tyres developed a puncture at a place called Khatauli. After getting it fixed, they proceeded on their way and reached Muzaffanagar in the evening. Reservations had been made at the dak bungalow by Kishan Singh who had written a letter to the caretaker. Unfortunately, repairs were being carried out at the dak bungalow and they had a very uncomfortable stay there.

Dinner consisted of rice, curry and vegetable paties and was served by the caretaker. After eating, Baba and party went out in search of masts. Baidul took them to a village ten miles from Muzaffarnagar where Baba contacted a mast. This mast lived in a hut which was located in a sugar cane field on top of bamboo stilts. Baba had to climb a ladder to reach the hut and contact the mast.

After this, Baba contacted a highly advanced female mast named Allahdi, who was the spiritual chargeman of Muzaffarnagar. She was very old and had fractured her leg in an accident a few days earlier. One of her followers had taken her to his house and was looking after her. When Baba contacted her, she was lying on a cot. She was very happy to see Baba.

From there Baba proceeded to contact another powerful mast known as Kuttewala Baba. Kuttewala basically means one who has dogs. The mast got this peculiar name because he always kept four to five dogs of good breed with him. He lived in a nice house, wore good clothes and moved around in a car. Baba was successful in contacting him and, after the contact, they returned to the dak bungalow late in the night.

The next day, after morning tea, Baba left Muzaffarnagar. Their first halt was at Roorkee. About four miles from Roorkee, on the Haridwar road, there was a mazar (Shrine) of Hazarat Makdum Ali Alhmed Sabir, located in Piran Kalyar. He was a great muslim saint of the time. A legend says that he once went into a trance and was unable to come out of it. In order to bring him out, his master told the local people to bring in dancing girls and to organize a dance with loud music playing around the saint. The master was successful in his ploy and, in memory of that, every year a festival is held with dancing girls and loud music. Thousands of people from all over come to take part in it.

Baba, along with Baidul, Kaka Baria and Keki, went to the mazar where they circled the tomb seven times. When they came out, several fakirs (beggars) who were sitting outside the tomb, approached Baba for alms. One of the fakirs said, "Please give some alms to fakir." Hearing this, Baba pointed to His empty pocket and told Keki to tell the fakir, "We are also fakirs and our pockets are empty."

From Roorkee, Baba left for Pathri, a small place near the Ganges canal. On arrival, Baba and Baidul went to contact a mast who was lying in the sand on the banks of the canal. Baba asked Kaka Baria and Keki to stay back in the car. After completing the contact, Baba returned looking very happy. From here they departed for Haridwar.

Getting there, they first went to the refreshment room of the station. After freshening up, Baba and all had lunch. When they came out of the station, Baba spotted a mast just outside the main gate. The mast wanted to go for a ride in the car so Baba took him around the place. Baba gave the mast an orange to eat, but the mast refused and asked Baba to eat it. Baba told the mast that the orange was for him, after which the mast took it. Eventually, Baba dropped the mast at the spot where they had picked him up and they all then proceeded to Rishikesh.

BABA CONTACTS NILKANTHWALA BABA

Baba and His companions parked the car on the banks of the Ganges when they reached Rishikesh. Baba wanted to contact Nilkanthwala Baba. This mast was the spiritual chargeman of the whole of Northern India and lived in a small cave on the top of a hill known as Nilkanth Pahad.

Kaka Baria wasn't well, so Baba asked him to stay back in the car. Baba, along with Baidul and Keki, set out in search of the mast. To reach him, they had to first cross the Ganges by boat. Next they had to pass through a forest. Baidul led the way and Baba and Keki followed him. As they were passing through the forest, Baba stopped and picked up three pebbles and threw them in three different directions. Looking at Keki, Baba said that the forest was known for wild elephants and they would often go on a rampage, attacking nearby villages. Keki understood that by throwing pebbles in three directions, Baba was keeping the wild elephants at bay.

Finally, they reached the cave where the mast was residing. On entering, they found that the cave was empty except for an earthen water pot and a cot on which the mast was lying naked. Two old women devotees were sitting by the mast's side, pressing his legs.

When they entered the cave, the women

moved aside. Baba sat in the dust near the cot and began pressing the feet of the mast. It was a unique scenario. The mast was sleeping on the cot like a king and Baba, who was the emperor of all emperors, was pressing the mast's feet like a slave. Truly He was the slave of the love of His lovers.

After some time, Baba wanted to depart, but the mast refused to let Him go. When Baba requested a second time, the mast refused again. The third time, however, when Baba asked the mast for his permission to leave, the mast clapped and gave permission. Baba asked Baidul and Keki to take darshan of the mast and then they left.

When they returned to the river, there was no boat and Baba, the All knowing God-Man, playing the part of an ordinary man, expressed concern as to how they would now cross the river. He even showed how helpless He was feeling under the circumstances.

When, after some time had passed, the boat came, Baba looked relieved. The boat service was run by a charitable trust and it was free. However, on reaching the other side, Baba asked Keki to give the boat man two annas. After this, Baba and all left for Dehra

Baba asked Keki to have dinner with Him. After dinner, Keki went to sleep at Nalawala's place which was located opposite Baba's bungalow. Baba asked Freiny Nalawala to prepare breakfast for Keki and to send the same to the bungalow for Baba who wanted Keki to have his breakfast with Him before leaving for Delhi. Baba paid Freiny for the breakfast.

The next morning, Freiny prepared a breakfast of omelet and bread and sent it to Baba's place. When Keki was served, he waited for Baba to come before eating. Baba came and asked what the breakfast was. Then Baba broke off a small piece of the omelet and ate it. While doing so, He commented, "Nazar Nu," which basically means "bad sight."

By eating a small piece, Baba had removed any bad sight that could have fallen on the meal by any stranger looking at it. In India it's commonly believed that if a strange person looks at your meal or looks at you with envy, then the so-called bad sight of that person could harm you. So people often offer a tiny amount of food from their plate to the birds or animals in order to break the bad sight.

After eating a small piece, Baba gave the rest to Keki to eat. Baba then asked Keki to leave for Delhi and to·send Him a telegram of his safe arrival when he got there.

SAINT KICKS NILKANTHWALA BABA

In Haridwar, near the banks of the river Ganges was a Shiva Ashram. This Ashram was run by a saintly person. He was well known throught the town and worshipped by many . Daily this saint would feed hundreds of people. Outside his ashram there was a Banyan tree under which a cot was placed, where the saint would sit or lie down and his devotees would be around him. It was called as the saint's Gaadi (throne) by the devotees.

It so happened that one day Nilkanthwala Baba was passing by . Seeing the mast, who was completely naked , the saint became curious and called him. When Nilkanthwala Baba came near, the saint didn't sit on the ground as the other devotees did. Instead he sat on the table which was placed near the Saint's cot. In India it is a tradition to sit a level lower than the saint. One cannot sit on the same level as the saint. So out of respect for the saint, people would generally sit on the floor. Seeing Nilkanthwala Baba sit on the table, which was at a higher level than the cot on which the saint was, made the saint furious.

Nevertheless the saint put up with the disrespect shown to him by the mast and enquired of him as to where he had come from. Nilkanthwala Baba, instead of answering, started abusing the saint and all the deities. The saint couldn't take it anymore and dragged the mast away. Took him a distance and kicked the mast with his right foot. Nilkanthwala Baba laughed and went away.

When the saint returned to his Gaadi, he realized that his right foot was going numb. The numbness kept increasing and within a few hours his leg was paralyzed. Doctors were called and medical treatment was given to the saint, but there was no improvement. As time passed by and all treatments failed to cure the condition, the saint realized that it was because he had kicked the mast that this had befallen him. He realized that Nilkanthwala Baba must have been a spiritually advanced soul and regretted his actions. He started looking out for the mast but the mast was nowhere to be seen. Nilkanthwala Baba would stay at Haridwar for sometime and then move to Rishikesh where he would spend few days.

After about one and half months, the saint saw Nilkanthwala Baba. Dragging his right foot, he approached the mast and requested him to undo what he had done by curing his right leg. Nilkanthwala Baba pretended that he knew nothing and had done nothing. The saint pleaded and said "I know it is you who has done it because my leg got paralysed after I kicked you."

At this Nilkanthwala Baba asked, "Why did you kick me?" The saint begged for forgiveness and pleaded again. Nilkanthwala forgave the saint and told him to pray to God and it would go away. True enough the saint recovered. After this incident the saint would make Nilkanthwala Baba sit on the Gaadi and he himself would sit on the floor with his devotees. In this manner hundreds of Sadhus who were the followers of the saint now began to worship Nilkanthwala Baba.

It is for this reason that Baba would often warn that, "A mast shouldn't be disturbed or troubled for if he were to curse you then you would be doomed for life."

NILKANTHWALA GOES TO BABA

A few months before Nilkanthwala Baba passed away, Baba asked Shatrugan Kumar to bring him to Meherazad. At that time, Nilkanthwala Baba was in Rishikesh. Kumar went to Rishikesh with the intention of bringing the mast. He knew where the mast resided. On reaching the place, Kumar found that the mast was not in his room. Upon inquiring with the local devotees, Kumar was told that the mast was in a very angry mood since morning and had stormed out of his room. Kumar went in search of the mast and finally located him in a tiny abandoned hut.

On seeing Kumar, the mast came out of the hut. He grabbed Kumar's hand and said, "I have been waiting for you." Kumar told the mast "Baba I have come to take you with me." Seeing Kumar interact with the mast, some local devotees of the mast gathered around him. When they realized that Kumar was trying to take the mast away, they protested. Kumar told the crowd very firmly, "If Nilkanthwala Baba chooses to come with me willingly, then you cannot stop us so let us ask him." Kumar asked the mast "Baba, I have come to take you to Meher Baba, do you wish to come with me?" The mast expressed his willingness and the crowd let him go.

While taking the mast, Kumar had to travel some distance by bus. As Nilkanthwala Baba was completely naked, some of the passengers objected. Even the bus conductor was upset. Kumar tried explaining to them that the mast was a God-Intoxicated soul and was revered in Rishikesh, however they were not pacified. Kumar then thought of a plan. Nilkanthwala Baba carried a brass bowl with him, wherever he went. It was the only thing he possessed and he never parted with it. Kumar turned to the mast and said " Baba there are many thieves in this bus. They want to steal your brass bowl. See how they are staring at it." On hearing this, the mast took the bowl and clasped it between his thighs with his two hands, just like a child holding onto something precious. In this way the mast's nakedness was covered by the bowl and the rest of the journey was peaceful.

On reaching Meherazad Kumar took the mast to Baba. During their stay at Meherazad, Baba did his work with the mast. When the work was finished, Baba asked Kumar to take the mast back. Nilkanthwala Baba pleaded with Baba to not send him back. He wanted to stay with Baba. Baba assured the mast that he would call him very shortly. With sadness in his eyes, the mast left Baba. A few months later the mast passed away. True to the promise, Baba called the mast to Him in order to live with Him forever.

KEKI'S PREDICTION COMES TRUE

For more than a year I had to make frequent trips to Delhi to attend to the case filed by Meherazad Free Dispensary against the polluting Chemical Factory which was going on in the Supreme Court of India. This was in the year 1994 – 1995 . During this period I frequently visited Keki Desai as he lived a short distance away from the Parsi Dharmshala where I was living.

It so happened that a Baba lover named Anil Sharma worked as a Supreme Court clerk. Whenever our case was listed for hearing in the court, he too would try to come for the hearing. One Saturday after the Court working hours were over, he told me that he was going to meet Keki Desai and asked me if I wanted to go with him. Anil visited Keki almost every Saturday. As the Mandali were constantly pressuring me to visit Keki, I went with him. I was happy that he was taking me as I did not know my way around.

As I got to know Keki better I began to like him immensely. He had lots of Baba stories to share and also had a trunk load of Baba souvenirs which he showed us and allowed us to touch. He took great interest in the Chemical factory fight and enquired regularly about its progress. He would enquire about all the Mandali's health and would frequently send through me some special Delhi snacks which the

Mandali liked.

Often when it looked that the Chemical factory fight was not progressing, it was Keki's confidence that kept my spirits high. He was one of the very few people who had a strong conviction that Baba would shut the industry down, no matter how powerfully connected the owner was. He would tell me often, "The factory owner does not realize who the Mandali are. They are not ordinary souls. For the suffering that he has caused to the Mandali, he will definitely have to pay the price. He is playing around with fire and he thinks he will get away with it, as nothing has happened to him so far. However in the end the fire will burn him down completely and reduce him to ashes."

Surprisingly, even the Mandali didn't have that confidence, for we had already been dismissed by the High Court Judges, who didn't consider our case. It was rejected on technical ground – of disputed facts. Keki's confidence was one more reason why I sought his company.

Unfortunately Keki passed away on 2nd Dec 1994. However, before that he inquired with Anil as to when I was coming to Delhi for the case. When Anil gave him the date, Keki told him "Rustom, when he comes next time, his trip will be a waste, but after that on his next trip Baba will perform His miracle."

What inspired Keki to say such a thing no one knows but it happened exactly as he said. I came to Delhi but our case never came up for hearing but at the next hearing the judges were upset at the delaying tactics of the owner and closed him down permanently. Our advocate was very happy with the results and commented, "It is a fabulous order. Your Meher Baba has truly performed a miracle." Although this order came in Feb of 1995, when Keki was no more, it seems that he had already seen the order with his inner sight and knew its content.

Made in the USA
Columbia, SC
08 December 2021

50675438R00113